DEVIL'S BREATH

SYDNEY RYE MYSTERIES
BOOK 5

EMILY KIMELMAN

The Devil's Breath
Sydney Rye Mysteries, Book 5
Copyright © 2013 by Emily Kimelman

All rights reserved.
No part of this book may be reproduced in any form or by any electronic or mechanical means, including information storage and retrieval systems, without written permission from the author, except for the use of brief quotations in a book review.

The author expressly prohibits any entity from using this publication for purposes of training artificial intelligence (AI) technologies to generate text, including without limitation technologies that are capable of generating works in the same style or genre as this publication. The author reserves all rights to license uses of this work for generative AI training and development of machine learning language models.

Heading illustration: Autumn Whitehurst
Cover Design: Christian Bentulan
Formatting: Jamie Davis

For my brother, Sam, who I love very much

*I can't run no more
with that lawless crowd
while the killers in high places
say their prayers out loud.
But they've summoned, they've summoned up
a thundercloud
and they're going to hear from me.*
—Leonard Cohen "Anthem"

CHAPTER ONE
LONG DAY'S JOURNEY INTO NIGHT

At the end of a long journey, lightning flashed outside my window...*I need more control.*

My hand jumped to Mulberry's forearm and squeezed. Shutting my eyes, I struggled not to picture the small plane cracking in half, my body flying through the air, still seat-belted to the beige leather chair; Blue, his paws grasping at empty space, disappearing into the bruise-colored clouds.

The small jet shook and our pilot's voice, smooth and steady, came over the loudspeaker, "Sorry about the bumps. We'll have you down in Miami in about twenty minutes. Just hold tight."

Mulberry put his hand over mine. "Don't worry," he said. "We'll be there soon."

He smiled, making his crow's feet crinkle. Mulberry's eyes were deep emerald with ochre and flashes of gold. I tried to smile back but could tell I was just giving a grimace. Mulberry handed me his whiskey and soda. I finished it off.

The ice cubes danced in my empty glass. Then we were suddenly out of the clouds. Below us the ocean was close, steel blue with white caps cresting each wave. The city's skyscrapers looked like towers of mercury in the storm's eerie light. Raindrops clung to my window, streaking across it as our speed pushed them aside.

Hugh was somewhere down there in that city, a flat landscape made multi-dimensional through the efforts of man. My stomach lurched as we dropped through the air, my seat belt pressing into me. Blue whined softly and flattened himself even further onto the floor of the plane.

A giant of a dog, Blue has the coat of a wolf, the snout of a Collie, with one brown eye and one blue. Both of which were trained on me at that moment. My fear was freaking him out. Closing my eyes, I tried to imagine the turbulence as a gentle rocking, but it didn't work. An ice cube jumped out of my glass, landing on the carpeting. Blue, his belly still flat on the ground, inched his way toward it, then his tongue stretched out and pulled the cube into his mouth. He crunched twice before looking back up at me, now hoping for more whiskey-flavored ice. I couldn't help but smile at the expectant look on his fuzzy face.

We touched down with a jerk that sent my heart racing one more time. But as we slowly taxied toward our hangar, the storm seemed suddenly minor. Just a breath of wind fluttered across the puddles, turning them into shimmering mirrors framed by the dark tarmac.

"All right Ms. Rye," our captain's voice came back on over the loudspeaker. "Sorry about that descent, but we got you here safe. Thanks for flying with us, I hope we'll have you back real soon."

As soon as humanly possible. I didn't want to be here, but Hugh was in trouble, and if there was one person I cared about in this world it was him. He was a tie to my murdered brother, a shared memory bank. I would do anything to help Hugh.

I wondered what his reaction would be when he saw me. The world thought I was dead. Somehow I felt that Hugh would know I wasn't. It was possible, I recognized, that the guilt of not letting him know I was alive gave me unrealistic hopes.

Robert Maxim was waiting in the hangar. I stopped at the top of the steps and looked down at him. He smiled, his eyes brightening. Maxim was taller than Mulberry but not as broad, more lean and fluid. Robert's rich brown hair was turning a brilliant silver at the temples. "You're looking a little green," he said as I made my way down the steps, his eyes picking up the blue in his tie and twinkling at me. Like we were friends. Like he never tried to kill me.

"And you're looking a little orange," I answered, referring to the man's tan.

He laughed deeply, the sound bouncing around in the large hangar. Behind Robert, a tall man dressed in a dark suit and wearing a driver's cap stood in front of a sleek black limo. Robert turned to him. "Claude," he waved the man over. Claude looked like a Claude, like a character from a kickboxing movie. The one with the scar across his chest and mammoth reach. But, who, of course, is bested by our plucky hero, or heroine as the case may be. "He can take your luggage," Robert said.

I held up my small duffel. "This is all I've got."

Robert raised an eyebrow. "I love a woman who travels light."

"Bobby," Mulberry said, reaching out his hand.

Maxim took it and shook, smiling. "You got our girl back," he said to Mulberry.

I bristled but bit my tongue. Without Maxim's intervention I wouldn't know Hugh was in trouble. But that didn't mean I was their "girl" or that I was "back".

Claude took my bag and opened the door for me. I climbed in, scooting to the far bench so that my back was against the driver's seat. Blue followed me, turning so that he could settle his side against my legs and face the door. Mulberry came next, his broad shoulders making it hard for him to maneuver in the narrow space. I flashed back to last night, his thick arms and rough hands holding my hips, and felt a blush creep up my neck. He smiled as he sat on the bench to my left, which faced the bar. I turned to the row of liquor bottles, busying myself making another whiskey and soda. Bobby sat closest to the door facing me across the long expanse of space.

A fresh drink in my hand I sat back into the soft black leather as the car rolled out of the private airport. "Does Hugh know I'm alive?" I asked.

Bobby shrugged. "I didn't tell him."

"Where is he?"

"At his apartment. We can go there now if you want."

"Yes," I said and then turned away from him, looking through the tinted windows. Puddles swelled around sewer drains. As we passed through them, our car pushed waves onto the sidewalks as high as people's calves. Pedestrians hurried through the mess, raising their knees high and clutching umbrellas with white knuckles. We stopped at a light and I watched one man who stood on the corner, his face tilted toward the receding clouds, arms loose at his sides, ignoring the foaming gray-green water that swirled around his ankles.

As crazy as me...

CHAPTER TWO
HUGH

Hugh lived in a high-rise on an island. The building stretched up into the clearing sky, reflecting back the blues and silvers of the receding clouds and still turbulent sea. We cruised past the front entrance and pulled into a garage. It was gray and fluorescent-lit, grimy and stale. Claude stopped in front of a door spray painted with the number one. Robert climbed out, followed by Mulberry. Blue and I were last. Mulberry went to open the door but I told him to wait.

Robert flicked his eyes to me. "Yes?" he said

"I don't want to sound fucked up here but, Robert, I do not trust you."

"No?"

I looked over at Mulberry. "I'm not insane here." He shrugged. I turned back to Robert. "You. Tried. To. Kill. Me."

"I'm trying to make that up to you," he said evenly. "I thought you understood."

"Make up to me that you tried to actually kill me?"

"You asked me to."

"No, no," I shook my head, anger rising in me. "I asked you to fake Joy Humbolt's death. You tried to shoot Sydney Rye. Big mistake. Huge."

Bobby nodded and raised his wrist, looking at his watch. It was simple with a gold face and thin leather strap. The timepiece looked understated against his deeply tan skin. "I understand your position," he said. "I had hoped you would see my intervention in this matter as a favor." He looked over at Mulberry. "But I can see you have not thought this through."

I laughed. "Uh, I've thought it through." I yanked up the hem of my skirt and exposed the thick scar that slashed across my thigh. "Just like the bullet went through."

Bobby looked at my exposed thigh and wet his lips. I pulled my dress back down quickly, feeling my neck flush with anger and shame. His eyes roved up my body, lips parting into a smile at the blush on my neck. I held his gaze and concentrated on breathing steadily. "I think it's time for you to leave."

"At least let me escort you upstairs," he said.

"I can walk her up," Mulberry said.

Robert turned to me. "You trust him? You know he trusts *me*," Maxim practically purred at me.

"You can go too, Mulberry," I said, not breaking my gaze from Robert's.

Mulberry didn't argue.

"Who will you tell the front desk is calling? Hugh's never heard of Sydney Rye," Robert said. "Let us take you up and then we'll both leave. How's that sound?"

"Fine," I said, realizing he was right.

EK

The lobby was sparse with modern black leather couches and fresh flowers. My sandals barely made a sound as I walked over the white marble floor but Bobby's hard dress shoes sent echoes through the space. A woman, about twenty-five, blonde, sun-kissed, and smiling, sat behind the reception desk wearing a white button-down shirt and a name tag that read "Brandy".

"We're here to see Hugh Defry," Mulberry said, leaning an arm on the chest-high desk.

Brandy smiled picking up the phone. "Who should I say is calling?" she asked.

"Robert Maxim," Bobby said.

She nodded and dialed. I could hear the ringing on the line. It sounded far away and old-fashioned. A click, a muffled hello, and then Brandy was announcing Robert. I held my breath as she nodded. "Go on up," she said.

Maxim lead the way to the bank of elevators. I felt pressure building in my chest as we rose to the 28th floor. The lift opened onto a carpeted hallway. Black and white photographs of the ocean hung between each apartment door. In some it raged, sputtering froth and spray against rocks, and in others the sea undulated gently to the horizon, looking smooth and friendly.

Robert knocked and I heard movement on the far side of the door. I gripped my hands into fists and licked my lips, anxiety churning in my chest. And then there he was. Hugh. A little over six feet tall with broad, lean shoulders, a wide and open face, he was a good looking guy. My brother had good taste. Hugh's baby blue eyes were bloodshot and dark circles hung beneath them. A light blond stubble grew on his jaw. He nodded to Robert and then his gaze fell on me. He started, stepping back slightly, his eyes widening. "Joy?" he whispered.

I nodded without speaking. Blue recognized Hugh too, and wagged his tail enthusiastically, letting out a growl of excitement and then a quick, high-pitched bark. Hugh's eyes dropped to look at him. "Blue," he said, shaking his head.

At the sound of his name Blue wagged his whole body over to Hugh and bent his head, pushing against Hugh's leg, then flipped himself around so that he was sitting on Hugh's foot looking up at him adoringly. Hugh reached down and pet him. Blue closed his eyes and sighed appreciatively.

Hugh looked up. "You're alive," he said, his voice breaking as tears rose into his already devastated eyes.

I stepped toward him tentatively, but then he held out his arms and I fell into them, squeezing Blue between us. Closing my eyes, I felt Hugh's breath on my shoulder and the beat of his heart against my breast. Hugh pulled back first and held me at arms length, looking down at my face. I swiped at a tear and smiled.

Wrapping his arm around my shoulders, Hugh turned into the apartment. I took a deep breath, smelling baking bread, and my stomach churned with excitement and long-repressed memories of a happier time. We navigated down a narrow hall and then the apartment opened up into a large, light-filled living room. Through the floor-to-ceiling windows I could see small homes laid out in a grid, their tile roofs orange and cheerful compared to the restless ocean and quickly moving clouds. "Wow," I said. "This place is amazing."

Hugh smiled and squeezed my shoulder. "Thanks."

"Smells good in here," Mulberry said.

Hugh's eyes widened. "My bread," he said before hurrying toward the open kitchen to our left. He opened one of two ovens recessed into the wall and, grabbing hot mitts from the Corian countertop, pulled out a loaf pan and placed it next to the sink.

I just stared at Hugh as he moved around his kitchen. I still couldn't really believe that he was here in front of me. And I couldn't understand why I'd stayed away so long.

EK

I followed Hugh into the kitchen and watched as he pulled out a second loaf. On the counter was a fruit bowl I recognized and the memory of it jerked the breath from me.

James made it in a pottery class, one of his lesser talents. He was a brilliant illustrator and designer, but when it came to three-dimensional work, his skills fell apart. And yet, here, on Hugh's counter, was one of those lopsided creations, the glaze glistening deep blue in the sunlight.

As I reached out to touch it I saw a photograph on the wall. Framed in dark wood James, Hugh, and I smiled at the camera. The rough Atlantic crashed behind us, our hair wet and sandy. I could almost smell the sunscreen on our skin and the beer on our breath.

My smile was so big that my eyes were practically closed. Long hair, bright blonde in the sea sunshine, hung past my breasts. James's arm was flung lazily across my shoulders and he caught the camera with his gray eyes, holding its gaze, unafraid, happy, alive.

I turned back to Hugh and he looked at me, smiling. How did he even recognize me? My hair, shorter and with long bangs, was dyed with henna to a deep copper. The scar under my left eye puckered pink. The line of tissue that ran above my eyebrow was covered by the bangs that drifted into my gray eyes, so much colder than they used to be. My body was taut and balanced, always on edge, ready for a fight, sculpted for protection. The difference between me and the girl in that picture seemed unfathomably vast. Almost as if it was impossible we'd ever been the same.

How much had Hugh changed? I thought of the crime scene photos I'd looked at with Mulberry on the flight. The close-ups of blood splattered across pinstriped bed sheets. Lawrence Taggert's ripped fingernails. The way his suit jacket floated around him as he lay face down, trapped between the roots of an everglade apple tree. Did Hugh knock him out? Lock the man in his trunk? Ignore his pleas for mercy and incessant banging while he drove to the swamp? Where Hugh then pushed Lawrence to his knees and shot him between the eyes? Finally kicking his corpse into the water for the gators to eat?

Hugh reached across the kitchen counter and took my hands. Perhaps his scars weren't on his face. But there must be something left of those people in that photograph. I glanced back at it. Hugh stood on the other side of James, his hand wrapped around James's hip. He grinned at the camera, his smile full of youthful exuberance and a touch of alcoholic euphoria. His dirty blond hair was pushed off his forehead and sand coated one bare shoulder. Was James the only ghost in that picture?

Hugh followed my gaze to the photograph. "That was a fun day," he said.

"Yeah," I agreed, turning to him.

"It's good to see you," he smiled.

"It's good to see you, too," I said, feeling close to him. No matter how far we traveled and changed there was an unbreakable tie between us.

Perhaps there was a little left of that girl in the picture. I hoped that Hugh hadn't changed as much as me.

Bobby cleared his throat and we both turned to him. He stood next to Mulberry, his fitted suit sleek and dangerous-looking compared to Mulberry's rumpled jeans and white linen shirt.

"We will give you two some time to catch up," he said. And with a small bow Robert turned, Mulberry with him, and left.

EK

"We should have a drink," Hugh said, grabbing a bottle of whiskey out of a cabinet and turning toward me.

I nodded my agreement. He grabbed two glasses off an exposed shelf above the sink, then splashed whiskey into them. He passed me one. I took it, and Hugh leaned his hip against the counter. "God, so much has changed, Joy. Everything." His face tightened. "How did we get here?"

I sipped the whiskey, it was warm and burned my mouth, filling my sinuses with its powerful smoky scent. "I don't know."

Blue barked. I turned to him; he looked at the sink, then back at me. "Oh, sorry, boy. Hugh, can I have a bowl for water?"

"Yeah, of course, sure." Hugh put down his drink and opened a bottom drawer to pull out a bowl. Filling it with water from the tap he placed it on the floor for Blue, who lapped at it.

"Did you really kill Kurt Jessup?" Hugh asked gently as he returned to his full height. Jessup, the man who murdered my brother, the maniac Robert Maxim let run wild, protected, and eventually killed.

I shook my head. "No, but it wasn't from a lack of trying." Hugh frowned. "He was already dead when I got there."

"But everyone in the world thinks you did it. Why haven't you denied it?"

Ignoring his question I asked one of my own. "Did you kill Lawrence Taggert?"

"No, I don't think so. I never wanted to. I don't know," Hugh turned away from me, placing both hands on the counter and looking out the giant windows. "I can't remember anything. This is so out of control."

I sipped my whiskey and then put it down on the counter next to me. "I can help you, don't worry," I said, placing my hand over his. He looked down at me, his blue eyes filled with tears.

"How?" he asked and his eyebrows raised. "How are you even here? I thought you were dead, Joy!" His voice hiccuped and Hugh turned away from me.

I looked at his profile and watched his Adam's apple bounce in his throat. "I'm sorry," I said.

"You said you'd call," he answered, his voice stronger, almost angry.

"I know." I wet my lips. "I should have, but..."

"What?" he asked, turning to me. "Why didn't you just let me know you were alive?" He shook his head, his eyes filling with disgust. "How could you let me think I'd lost you too, Joy?"

"That's the thing," I said, grabbing at his hand as he tried to pull it away. "I'm not Joy anymore, Hugh. My name is Sydney Rye, and I don't think you want to know me, but the fact is that you're in trouble and I can help you. I'm not going to let anyone hurt you."

He pulled free from me. "You already hurt me," he yelled, backing away.

"Hugh - " I reached across the counter for him, but he stepped further away.

"Don't, Joy."

"My name is Sydney now. Trust me Hugh, you need me. I think you're in even deeper shit than you realize."

"What?"

"I'm almost positive Robert Maxim is behind all of this. I think he set you up to lure me back here. Hugh, I think we're both in a shit ton of danger, and my suggestion is fleeing. We need to go before they have a chance to realize we're gone. We need to go now."

Hugh stared at me, his face dropping, the anger and hurt draining away. "I don't understand."

"And I don't think there is time to explain." I glanced around the apartment. James's fruit bowl, the paintings on the walls, the cookbooks that lined the kitchen shelves, pots and pans suspended above a six burner stove. How could I explain that he would have to leave all this behind because of me? "You'll be able to come back," I decided. "But we've got to go now."

"Why does Robert Maxim care about you?"

I came around the counter and took Hugh by the shoulders. "Listen to me," I bit my lip feeling the rough edge of my teeth as I raked them across the sensitive flesh. "This is my fault. I never should have gotten involved in New York. I got James killed and then I stupidly tried to avenge his murder without any concept of what was going on, the bigger picture. Do you understand?" I realized I was rambling. "The point, Hugh, is that I've learned a lot since then. And one thing I know for sure is Robert Maxim is dangerous."

Hugh moved away from me. "Who are you?"

"Sydney Rye, Hugh, and we need to go."

"This doesn't make any sense. My lawyer recommended Fortress Global Investigations. He said they were the best."

"They are, so let me ask you this: if Robert isn't behind all this why is the head of the company working on this case?"

"It's pretty high profile," he said. "Lawrence and I are both minor celebrities." Hugh had partnered with Lawrence on his restaurant *Defry* after winning the cooking competition *Sliced*, which Lawrence produced.

"This is my fault, Hugh," I said. "Please let me help you."

Hugh bit his lip. "I think," he blinked. "I think it's like lightning. You know how if you're struck by lightning it's more likely to happen again."

"Hugh, what are you talking about?" I asked.

He shook his head slightly and wet his lips again. "I think that violence is like lightning. If you get struck once you're more likely to be hit again."

"Hugh, I brought this here."

"A lightning rod?" he said with a weak smile.

"Please," I started again, but he cut me off.

"I'm not going to run away. I need to know what happened."

"Hugh, just… Just trust me, please."

"Joy -"

"Sydney."

"Fine, Sydney." He took a breath. "I'm not running away. I have to find out what happened. Don't you understand? I have no idea what happened." Tears sprang to his eyes again.

"I'm sorry," I said. Watching him cry broke something inside of me and the wall of bluster and fight that kept me alive seemed to crumble under its weight. "We'll find out," I promised.

"So you'll stay?"

EK

Blue left my side, and I felt a chill where the dog's warmth usually touched me, against the scar on my thigh. I watched him move quickly but quietly across the room until he stood at the end of the hall with a clear view to the front door. Hugh followed my gaze, and in the silence I heard footsteps approaching.

Blue's hackles raised off his shoulder and back, changing his appearance from something slick and powerful to a wooly, gigantic beast. A sound at the door and his lips pulled back from sharp, bone white canines. As I heard the doorknob turn Blue growled in a pitch so low it was almost just a vibration humming through the air.

The whoosh of the door opening was quickly followed by an "Oh shit" and the door slamming.

"That's my friend," Hugh said, pointing at the door.

Hugh's phone rang and he grabbed it up off the counter, hitting the speaker button. "Santiago, I'm sorry—"

"Oh thank Jesus, you're okay. Hugh," the speaker took a quick breath, "I don't know how to tell you this. But," he paused for a moment and then blurted out, "there is some kind of wolf in your house. It may be a zombie. I don't know. Thing is scary!"

Hugh motioned at Blue, waving his arm, signaling for me to *do something*. "Blue," I said, "it's okay." He turned and looked at me, lowering his lips and deflating his hackles. They remained a bit puffed, but they would smooth soon. "Come." Blue hurried to my side, his tail wagging, looking the picture of a normal, happy, giant, zombie wolf.

"You can come in," Hugh said into the phone as he crossed the living room toward the entrance. I heard the door open again and followed

Hugh to greet our guest, Blue back in place by my side. "I'm so sorry," Hugh said as a tall man with dark, short cropped hair, a strong jaw line, wearing a white T-shirt and jeans walked in holding his phone and ladened with grocery bags .

"What is going on?" he asked. "Corazon, I thought something happened to you."

Hugh smiled and leaned forward, kissing the man on the cheek then took some of the shopping bags from him. "Hi," I said. "Sorry Blue gave you a scare. He can be protective."

Santiago looked down at Blue. "As long as he listens to you, I don't mind. He isn't really hungry for human blood is he?" Santiago asked, a playful twinkle in his eye.

"No," I said, smiling. "I'm Sydney Rye," I continued, extending my hand. "I'm working with FGI on Hugh's case."

Santiago raised his eyebrows and shook my hand. "You're a detective?" he asked, eyeing me up and down.

"Yes," I said, reaching down to pull at my skirt. "I just got off a plane," I continued and reached up to touch my hair, feeling it was a mess.

"You're here to help with Hugh's case. Fantastico." Santiago gave me a dazzling smile and I realized how gorgeous he was, then I wondered if this was Hugh's boyfriend, then I wondered how I felt about that. While I stood there thinking, Santiago continued into the kitchen and placed the bags on the counter. He began to unload the first one but paused. "Wait," he said, looking over at the photo of Hugh, James, and me. He stared at our smiling faces for a second and then turned to look back at me. "Are you Joy?" he asked.

"No," I said. "My name is Sydney Rye."

Santiago cocked his head at the photo and then looked at Hugh who stared intently at his toes. "Hugh?" Santiago asked, drawing out his name, playing with it the way only a Colombian tongue can do.

He nodded. "It's her."

Santiago gave a little jump of excitement. "Oh. My. God. I knew you weren't dead. I knew it." He stepped toward me. "And you're here to help with Hugh." His eyes widened with the sudden realization. Before I could prepare, he embraced me in a bear hug. Santiago smelled like black pepper and leather. He shook us back and forth and squeezed. His body was hard and comforting. "I'm so glad you're here."

"Thanks," I said. It came out muffled against his shirt.

Santiago held me out at arm's length and then looked over at Hugh who smiled sheepishly at us.

EK

It turned out Santiago was not dating Hugh. They were friends. Period. They met in a victims support group in a church basement "under fluorescent lights," Santiago pointed out, gesturing toward me with his wine glass. "Or maybe something would have happened. Ah, Corazon, we'll never know," he said, swinging his head around to Hugh and batting his long, thick black lashes at him. Hugh laughed and the tension around his eyes seemed to ease as the sound escaped him.

"When I found out he knew the real Joy Humbolt, well, I just couldn't believe it," Santiago told me. "We are both on Joyful Justice, you know?"

I shrugged and turned away. Joyful Justice was the website that sprung up after my escape from New York. It was based on the idea that I was some brave warrior princess who avenged her brother's murder and exposed corruption at the highest levels when the truth was totally different. I got my brother killed, then I fucked up avenging him and got myself exiled. But the people on Joyful Justice thought Joy Humbolt was a hero. And while I'd met people through it, people who had helped me in my work and whom I now considered good friends, I knew it was dangerous. "I don't have anything to do with that," I told Santiago. "I'm Sydney Rye now. Really, it's not something I like to talk about."

Hugh, seeing my discomfort, changed the subject. He told me how he and Santiago had worked together at the restaurant Hugh had created with Lawrence. Santiago was Hugh's sous chef, "vitally important to the whole operation," Hugh told me. To which Santiago responded:

"He just likes looking at my ass."

They had both been there the night of the fire. The event that precipitated the fight on the street which was one of the last things Hugh remembered.

"Lawrence was crazed," Hugh said as we sat back from a meal of freshly made tortellini (Hugh and Santiago both agreed that making pasta was a great way to relieve stress). "He came at me, saying the whole thing was my fault and that I'd ruined the restaurant. I thought it was over the top. I mean, restaurant fires happen. I thought we'd be back up and running in no time, but he was out of his mind." Hugh shook his head and Santiago refilled his wine glass, emptying our second bottle.

"He left after screaming at me in front of our staff,"—Santiago nodded to that—"the paparazzi, and our guests. Totally inappropriate," Hugh said, picking up his glass and taking a quick sip. "But I certainly didn't want to kill him. I just don't understand."

"What happened next?"

"I sent the staff home and waited until the fire department let me back into the kitchen so that I could assess the damage myself. It wasn't that bad really, at least I didn't think so. While the overhead fire suppression system had failed, we kept several fire extinguishers in the kitchen so were able to put it out pretty quickly."

Santiago cut in. "There was no 'we' about it. Hugh ordered the staff out and put out the blaze himself."

Hugh laughed. "You make it sound so dramatic."

"It was," Santiago said as he stood up and headed to the kitchen. He grabbed another bottle of wine off the shelf and came back to the table. "Hugh is a good man, you know that, Joy."

"Call me Sydney," I said.

"Oh, yes, sorry. Sydney," he said with extravagant eyebrow movements.

"What happened next?" I asked Hugh.

"I called a couple of contractors and left messages about getting the work done. And I called our insurance company and reported the fire. By then it was probably around 9 at night. I headed home, exhausted. Lawrence called right as I was getting out of the shower and asked me to come over. He apologized and said he wanted to talk. I told him I was tired, but he insisted." Hugh took another sip of his wine. "So," he shrugged, "I drove over to his place." His lips pursed. "And pulling into his driveway is the last thing I remember until waking up with the police banging on my door." He looked toward his door and then took a glug of wine. "I let them in. I had no idea what happened. They asked to look around. It never occurred to me I'd done anything horrible." Tears filled his eyes and I reached a hand across the table covering his.

"Maybe you didn't," I said. "And if you did, it obviously wasn't you. Not the real you."

"Does that mean there is another me? One that kills people?"

"No," Santiago said emphatically. "Of course not! You were drugged or something. Right, Sydney?"

"Absolutely," I said, squeezing his hand.

He shook his head as if to clear it and smiled at me. "Tell me what's been going on with you? I'm sick of this topic."

I smiled, my cheeks struggling with the gesture. How could I explain myself? I didn't need drugs or blackouts to commit murder. All I needed was an excuse.

I sat back and picked up my wine, sipping it to buy myself some time. "I think the story is too long for tonight," I said. "It's late, and I've been traveling for days."

"Fine," Hugh said. "But before you go I want to know what's going on with you and Mulberry."

"Oh, who's Mulberry?" Santiago asked, his eyebrows dancing.

I couldn't help but laugh. Hugh turned to Santiago. "He's the detective who originally investigated James's death but was removed from the case for getting too close to the truth. And he's kind of a super hunk these days. I remember him being less cute and more stressed. Man looks like he's relaxed a bit," Hugh said, bringing his attention back to me. "And damn, girl, the way he looks at you. Talk about a blaze."

I laughed and blushed, taking a quick sip of my wine. "It's complicated," I answered honestly. "And I'm sorry, but I really do need to go." I stood up.

"You can stay here," Hugh said.

"While I love that idea, my stuff is probably back at the hotel and I need to touch base with Mulberry."

"You sure that's all you need to touch with him?" Santiago asked, dropping his voice.

I laughed again, feeling lighter just for the secret being out. Hugh walked me to the door and we embraced, leaning into each other, unwilling to let go again. "Don't worry," I told him. "I'm going to fix this."

CHAPTER THREE
RUN, RUN, RUN

Claude and his limo were waiting when Blue and I got down to the garage. He took me to a hotel in South Beach. The streets were teeming with well-dressed hard bodies looking for a good time. When Blue and I walked into the lobby of the hotel Robert had booked for us, a stylish woman about my age, but better dressed, led us to a suite with modern furnishings and that veneer of impersonality that every luxury hotel room in the world shares.

I slept deeply without dreams or worries, but the instant my eyes opened a shot of adrenaline pumped through me, saturating my vision with color and making my hands shake.

Checking the bedside clock I saw it was 6 am. I'd gotten almost six hours. Mulberry wouldn't come knocking for awhile. Blue jumped off the bed and stood next to me. He licked my hand and wagged his tail then backed up, and with ears flat to his head, looked at the door. "Want to go for a run?" I asked. He warbled deep in his throat. Blue followed close to me, tapping his wet nose against my hip. He was there as I brushed my teeth, found my jogging clothes, tied my shoes, drank a big glass of water, untangled my headphone cords, and finally walked out the door.

Mulberry stood in the hall. I looked up and down the passage.

"I was just about to knock," he said.

I shrugged. "So you weren't just standing out here all night, hoping to run into me?" I said with a smile.

He shook his head, his lips twitching with a laugh. "There is a strategy meeting at 9 in Fortress Global's Miami headquarters. I've got a car, we can go together."

"Okay, thanks," I said, looking past him toward the elevators, wanting to go for my jog, calm my thoughts.

Mulberry took a step closer. He was wearing jogging shorts and a T-shirt. "I know you've never worked on a team like this before, but there is no reason to be nervous."

I looked up at him. "I'm not nervous about working with a team, Mulberry. I'm worried about Bobby fucking Maxim driving a knife into my back. I really don't know why you're not."

"If he wanted you dead you would be."

"That's supposed to make me feel better?"

Mulberry looked up and down the empty hallway. "We shouldn't be talking here. Let's go in." He gestured to my door, his forearm brushing against my bare bicep. I could smell him, and I didn't want to be alone with him. His scent made me trust him, it made me remember him and how we were, but I didn't have room for that. Not for any of that.

When I made no move to let him in, Mulberry brushed the back of his fingers down my arm and gently held my elbow. "Sydney, I can't believe you don't trust me," he stepped closer. "After everything." He looked down at me and his eyes were large and warm. Mulberry brushed a strand of hair away from my cheek and cupped the back of my head.

The ding of the elevator broke me free, and I jumped back from him as a kid came screeching down the hall closely followed by a frazzled looking mother. "I'm going for a run," I said and turned to the emergency exit, Blue close to my side. Bursting through the door I took the steps two at a time. The sound of my sneakers thudding against the concrete echoed in the desolate space. I heard the door open and a second set of sneakers hit the steps, pounding after me.

I pushed out of the stairwell into a sand alley. The sun, hovering at the edge of the dunes, was at eye level and blinded me for a moment.

But I felt the soft grains under my feet, and digging in pushed forward. I headed north, running parallel with the beach. I could smell it, taste its sweet tang in the air, but vegetation and dunes blocked the Atlantic from my vision.

Pulling my cap down on my brow, I focused on the path as I ran. Mulberry was behind me. I could sense him as easily as the ocean—in some ways he felt as large and dangerous. I kept running, picking up my pace as I hit the paved path that curled along the coast. It was not crowded at this early hour but a steady stream of runners, rollerbladers, bikers, and skateboarders shared the path. Two young men, their bodies lean and lithe, balanced on skateboards using long, gondola-like staffs to push themselves forward. They chatted easily with each other. As the distance between us closed, their conversation faltered slightly when they saw Blue. "Whoa," I heard one of them say as we ran past.

The sun was hot and scorched my skin, sending stinging sweat into my eyes. We ran through shade and then sun, feeling the burn and then cool relief but no amount of outside stimulus was shaking the thoughts of Mulberry from my head.

I didn't know what to do. Every nerve ending in my body told me to trust him. To fall into his strong arms, burrow my head into his chest and accept his comfort, his help, and his companionship. However, an even stronger instinct, something almost primordial, told me to stay back, to never trust anyone that much. Especially someone who worked with a man I thought of as my sworn enemy. He'd taken so much from me, including satisfaction of killing my brother's murderer. Bobby Maxim got there first. I pumped my legs harder, hitting the pavement with each long stride as the anger built in my chest. The pure hate I felt sometimes frightened me and I ran faster, trying to outrun my nature. Outrun my past and every dirty secret that I kept hidden there.

My lungs on fire, legs aching for relief, I slowed my pace, taking deep breaths to calm the rapid fire hammering in my chest. I felt Mulberry behind me, could smell his sweat as he neared and pushed myself further, picking up speed again, desperate to keep away from him. Unsure of what to do, I did the only thing I'd ever been truly good at. I ran.

Taking a path onto the beach I pushed through the deep sand. My thighs burned. The ocean was before me, calm and gentle in the early light. The reflection of the low sun lit a path to the horizon, shimmering and exquisite. My mind began to let go of all that haunted me as it concentrated on the heat, the push, the fight of the run.

I turned away from the sea and back onto the paved path, sweat pouring off my brow, and searched for shade. Finding a tree, its palm leaves shading the path with large swaths of zebra stripes, I stopped. Turning around to face Mulberry I was not sure what to say. So I just stood there and let the beating of my heart chase the fear and uncertainty from my veins.

"Fuck, I thought you'd never stop," Mulberry said, resting his hands on his knees. "If there is one thing you're good at it's running."

"That's what I think I should be doing right now."

Mulberry squinted up at me. "Yeah." He stood and smiled. "I'm not surprised."

"Yeah, because you know me so well, right?"

"You want to take Hugh and run, but he won't go."

I threw my hands up and, turning away from Mulberry, went and sat on a stone wall that followed the path. Leaning my head back, I gripped at the edge. I thought about getting up and sprinting for the ocean, jumping in and letting the waves wash over me. At least then my face would be cold. "Here," Mulberry said, holding out a bottle of water. The sunlight refracted into glitter on the condensation.

While my pride did not want to take it, my hand went out and grabbed it. I drank deeply then cupped some in my palm for Blue who lapped at it quickly. "Thanks," I said, extending it back to Mulberry. He took it and leaned his head back to drink from the half empty container. I watched a bead of sweat trickle through his stubble down his neck and rest in the hollow of his throat. Standing up I stretched toward my toes, concentrating on the grain of the pavement.

"Can we talk now?" he asked.

"I don't know what to say." I reached around my ankles and leaned deeper into the stretch feeling the backs of my legs loosen.

"Say you trust me."

I stood up slowly. "I want to, but your relationship with Bobby Maxim makes you suspect, Mulberry. I thought that after what happened in Mexico you'd never work for him again."

"Sydney, I—" he pursed his lips. "It's complicated."

"You want me to trust you? I want to know why you trust him." I crossed my arms over my chest and Blue sat by my side. We had time.

The wind picked up and, looking west, I saw dark clouds churning over the waterfront hotels, the soft edges of their art deco design stark against the darkening sky. A rain droplet struck my cheek and then more came quickly, cold and refreshing.

"Sydney, let's go. I'll explain at the hotel."

"No," I turned to him. "I'm not afraid of a little rain."

"Are you afraid of being alone with me?" He stepped closer and I backed away instinctively. A smile spread across Mulberry's lips. "That's what I thought."

"You're not such hot shit," I said. "I might want to fuck you, but that doesn't mean I can trust you."

He took another step and I backed away, but the distance between us closed. "So you do want to again?" he asked quietly. The rain was coming faster now. People were abandoning the park and we were alone.

I shook my head stepping away from him, putting needed space between us. "I can't, not while you're working with him."

"What do I have to do to prove you can trust me?"

His T-shirt, wet from the rain, clung to his chest outlining the strong muscles underneath. I looked up at him, he reached for me again and I slid back, bumping against a tree. He came in close, and I tilted my face to look up into Mulberry's deep green eyes. "Kill him," I said.

"What?" His eyes narrowed.

"Kill Robert Maxim." I pushed off the tree bumping into him. "Then I'll trust you."

He grabbed my arm roughly. "Are you crazy?" he asked. The wind picked up and blew my wet hair across my face.

I stared up at him, hardening my gaze so that he knew I wasn't joking. "There is one way to solve this without having to run, and that's to stand and fight, something else I'm pretty fucking good at," I said.

Mulberry shook his head. "Not against him, Sydney, don't."

I smiled. "You're the one who asked to prove your trustworthiness."

Mulberry sighed and his grip loosened on my arm. "Sydney, I really don't think he wants to hurt you." He licked his lips and shrugged. "He thinks you're talented, all he wants is to be on your team."

I laughed.

Mulberry's eyes flashed and his grip tightened again on my arm. "You don't ever want to hear it but people admire you." He grabbed my other arm and pushed me back against the tree. The rain whipped harder than ever, bringing out goosebumps on my skin as the chilly rain soaked through my thin clothes. "I'll prove it to you," he said, his voice low and rough. "We'll find who is actually responsible for this crime, and then maybe you'll start to understand some things."

"Let go of me."

His fingers loosened but he didn't back off. "Promise me you won't do anything stupid for at least a week." When I didn't answer he leaned in even closer and I could feel the heat coming off him, my cold skin aching to be nearer.

"I'll give you a week," I said. "But if anything happens to Hugh, I'll hold you personally responsible."

Mulberry smiled with relief.

"You can back up now," I said.

His fingers turned gentle, his right hand roaming up my shoulder. As Mulberry went to cup my face again I ducked out from under him and started back toward the hotel keeping an easy pace, feeling the sting of cold rain against my cheeks. Blue tapped my hip to let me know he was there. I heard Mulberry's footsteps behind me, keeping beat with mine.

CHAPTER FOUR
FORTRESS GLOBAL

The Miami headquarters of FGI were in a tall, glass-walled, downtown skyscraper. The lobby's ceiling was high, and sunlight slanted through the front wall of windows in beams of bright yellow. Mulberry showed his ID to two men who stood behind a reception desk. Wires curled out of their ears and dark glasses obscured their eyes. They were prepared for our arrival and handed me an ID, still warm from the printer. The photo on it was from that day, I was wearing the same shirt. I stared down at it.

Mulberry took my arm and we walked to the elevators. I looked up at him. "Everyone who comes in gets photographed," Mulberry said, answering my unasked question.

I nodded. "Of course."

We rode up to the 33rd floor and walked into what looked like a normal, well-appointed office space. "Mr. Mulberry," said a middle-aged woman behind a dark wood desk. "They are waiting for you in conference room," she glanced at her computer screen, "three," she finished. "Do you want me to send in coffee?"

"Some bagels, please," he said.

"Yes, sir."

Mulberry took my elbow and gently led me down the hall. My

stomach rumbled at the thought of cream cheese on an everything bagel. I hadn't had anything like that for months. Not surprisingly I didn't run into good bagels in India. Mulberry stopped outside a wooden door and let go of me before pushing through.

The room was about 15 x 25 with wall-to-wall green carpeting. An oval conference table made of expensive wood gleamed in the center of the room. To our left, large windows looked out at another building, also made of glass and filled with people. Three whiteboards hung with photographs and marked up in neat black handwritten notes covered the far wall. Close to the windows, in front of the boards, was a podium.

Three people sat in large, wheeled, black leather chairs around the table. They all turned when we walked in and, upon recognizing Mulberry, they stood. Placing his hand into the small of my back Mulberry urged me forward. "Sydney," he said, "this is our team." The closest person was a handsome Hispanic man in a well-fitting suit that showed off his strong physique. "Antonio," Mulberry said, gesturing to the man. Antonio had thick black hair and olive, clear skin. His brown eyes were warm and rich.

He reached out a hand to me. I smiled and shook. It was rough in all the right places. "I'm looking forward to working with you, Ms. Rye," he said with just the slightest bit of an accent.

"Thanks, Antonio."

"I'm Ashley," said the only other woman in the room, reaching across the conference table to shake my hand, inadvertently (or maybe not) giving us all insight into the shape of her breasts as they pushed against the satin cap-sleeved button-down shirt she wore.

"Nice to meet you," I said, taking her delicate hand in my own. It was soft and I noticed her nails were painted a shade of gray not so different from my eyes.

"I've been looking forward to working with you since Mulberry told us you were joining our team." She gave me a broad smile showing off white, straight teeth that an orthodontist must have helped with.

"Thanks," I said, not sure what to do with the amount of admiration in the younger woman's big blue eyes. She flicked her glance to Mulberry and I saw a blush creep between her breasts.

"And last but not least, this is Hugh's lawyer, Tony Edwards." A big man with close cropped gray hair and twilight blue eyes reached his hand out toward me.

"Pleasure," he said. We shook and I smiled at him. There was something inherently charming about him. He looked healthy and thoughtful. If I were on a jury, I'd listen to him.

"Do you want to see those numbers I put together?" Ashley asked Mulberry.

"Yes," Mulberry said, walking around the table to join her. I gravitated toward the whiteboards with Blue by my side. The smell of magic board ink filled my nostrils as I looked over the crime scene photos. A wide shot of the bedroom where the initial attack took place showed a disheveled bed, its sheets half off the mattress, centered in a large and expensive, though gaudily, decorated room. A headshot of the victim showed Lawrence Taggert looking handsome, his green eyes sparkling out of a tan face, jaw still strong, lips full and spread into a welcoming smile, almost a laugh, as though the photographer had just said something funny.

Next to the headshot was a resume for the late Mr. Taggert. Restauranteur, television producer, real estate developer, the man had his fingers in a lot of pots. I wondered which one got him killed. While the crime appeared to look personal, as though Hugh and he got into a raging fight that ended in Taggert floating face down in the swamp, I knew that was impossible. If Bobby Maxim hadn't arranged this whole thing, then the killer, sneaky little fucker, was probably hiding in the man's background.

Continuing along the board I saw Hugh's mug shot. He looked terrible. Dark circles under his eyes and a white crust on his lips made him look years older. I turned back to the room and saw Ashley smiling up at Mulberry, her big blue eyes filled with admiration. Mulberry smiled back and leaned over her to take a closer look at her notebook. Ashley turned her face to look at him and I was almost positive she inhaled, her eyes fluttering.

"Blue," I said. His collar jingled as he turned his head to me. "Go make friends," I said, subtly pointing at Ashley.

Blue walked over to the young woman and pushed his muzzle into one of her hands. She turned toward him and laughed, reaching out to pat his head. But when she returned her attention to Mulberry, Blue scooted in close and rested his massive head on her lap. She smiled down at him and Mulberry stood up and walked to the front of the room next to me.

I snapped my fingers and Blue abandoned Ashley, moving quickly to my side. She looked after him and I smiled at her. Sensing I was being watched, I looked up and saw Bobby Maxim leaning in the doorway, his arms crossed and a knowing smile on his face. I quickly took a seat at the table and turned my attention to Mulberry, who remained standing. He looked from me to Bobby but didn't say anything.

EK

"I assume everyone has had time to look over the case files. Why don't we start with Antonio. Give us a timeline breakdown," Mulberry said.

Antonio stood and walked to the front of the room. Mulberry took the chair across from me. Blue sat close and rested his head on my lap. I placed a hand on him, petting his velvety brow. Turning to the podium Antonio picked up a small controller. The lights dimmed, the windows darkened, and a screen lowered in front of the white boards.

As the screen settled into place with a small clunk it came to life; a powerpoint presentation titled "Case #6155 Hugh Defry/Lawrence Taggert" loaded on the screen with just the slightest of flickers.

"Hugh Defry and Lawrence Taggert met three years ago when Defry was a contestant on the show *Sliced*," Antonio said. The screen showed a group shot of men and women all wearing chef's outfits, Hugh at the center. "The final episode where he bested rival Daniele Spencer with what became the signature dish at *Defry*, 'duck fat ochre fries,' was the highest-rated finale the show had ever seen and broke records for the Food Network.

"Taggert, a judge and producer on the show, partnered with Hugh that same year to open *Defry* in Miami Beach." An image of the restaurant, green awning, walls of windows pushed aside to allow the breeze to mingle among the guests, flashed on the screen.

"Visited by the famous," a picture of Hugh and Taggert on either side of a beautiful woman, all of them smiling widely, arms around each other. "And the infamous," Antonio continued. A photo of Taggert and a big man, his smile unpracticed, his suit not quite in style, faced the camera across a table, brandy snifters in front of them. "*Defry* was an instant hit, they had plans to expand rapidly into casinos and resorts, including locations in Las Vegas, Palm Springs, and New York."

My stomach tightened at the mention of New York. "While there were rumors that the two men had a fiery relationship, they could have easily been dismissed as tabloid fare until last week when a fire hit *Defry* setting off the course of events that brings us all here today."

A little dramatic, I thought.

Antonio squeezed the controller, changing the image on the screen. An open oven, matte black with soot damage spreading out from it like a starburst, darkening the pristine stainless steel countertops and hood which reflected almost white under the bright light of the crime scene photographer's flash. It looked collapsed, ruined, like an explosion, not just fire, had raged within.

"The fire marshal is saying that the grease trap was not cleaned properly. The kitchen's logs are missing, but according to staff we've interviewed, Hugh was obsessively tidy."

"Are you suggesting it could have been sabotage?" I asked.

Antonio turned to me, his deep brown eyes unreadable in the dull light. "Yes, that is one of the leads we are following."

I felt Mulberry looking at me and glanced toward him as the picture on the screen changed again. Mulberry returned his attention to the screen and I watched his profile for a moment, checking for tension in his jaw, tightness around his mouth, but saw no signs of upset. I played with one of Blue's ears and looked back to Antonio.

"The fire began at the beginning of dinner service with an explosion that miraculously did not injure anyone working in the kitchen. The built-in suppression system failed, allowing the fire to rage unchecked for more than five minutes during which Hugh ordered his staff to evacuate the restaurant and then, using a fire extinguisher he kept in the kitchen, put out the fire himself." Antonio turned back to his audience, his voice lowering. "The fire chief said it was a foolish but brave move that most likely saved thousands in property damage and possibly the lives of people in the upstairs apartment. Mulberry, Edwards, and I agree that this is key evidence of our client's level head and respect for human life."

I looked down at Blue and found his eyes closed and breathing even. On the edge of sleep, I thought.

"The fire department showed up seven minutes after the alarm sounded and took over fighting the fire at that time, though from the men I spoke to it was mostly out before their arrival. However, they double checked everything, spending approximately an hour and a half on site. Long enough, certainly, to see the fight that took place between our client, Hugh Defry, and the victim, Lawrence Taggert."

I looked up as the screen changed again to show Hugh and Lawrence toe-to-toe on the sidewalk in front of *Defry*. Hugh was in a chef's outfit, black and white checked pants, and a soot-stained white smock. Taggert wore a suit that rose up as he pushed his finger into Hugh's chest. His palms out and posture leaning back, Hugh looked down at the smaller man with an expression of surprised anger. "This photo was taken by one of the paparazzi who often hang out around the entrance of *Defry*," Antonio said. "Their confrontation was short and then Taggert returned to his car and left."

"According to witnesses, Defry sent the rest of his staff home and waited until he could get back into the restaurant. He thanked several of the firemen personally and, once allowed back inside, called contractors leaving messages about getting the kitchen fixed."

"Defry thinks he left the restaurant around 9 and received a phone call from Taggert soon after asking him to come over. Defry claims that Taggert said he wanted to apologize. Defry remembers nothing after the drive out to Taggert's residence."

"We spoke to Taggert's maid, Esmerelda Garcia, who confirms that Taggert's wife was out of town—she spends a lot of time away apparently. It was Esmerelda's night off, and she was staying with her mother."

A crime scene photo showed shards of a white and blue porcelain vase scattered on a dark blue carpet, the blood on the vase brown, the stains on the carpet black. "A confrontation between two people began in the front hall. Taggert ran toward his bedroom and the killer followed, picking up a vase on the way. Defry or somebody else, though Defry's fingerprints were found on the vase, hit Taggert hard enough to stun him. He fell onto the bed." The screen showed the large bed with its twisted sheets and blood spatter. "The attacker pulled him off by the ankles and dragged him back through the front hall." A photo of a white marble floor with a red drag mark curling across it and out the front door flashed on the screen.

"At some point during the drive out to the Everglades, Taggert woke up and attempted to free himself from the trunk." A close up of fingertips, torn and blue, almost abstract except for the undeniable outline of the nail bed. Another photo flashed, knuckles bruised and swollen. "Defry was at the wheel, as you can see from this surveillance film at a gas station on 8th Street." A video played of Hugh's BMW pulling up next to a pump, Hugh climbing out of the driver side and using his credit card to pay for the gas. He stared blankly down at the handle until it clicked off and then replaced it. You could see the trunk lid jumping as the man trapped inside fought for freedom. Too calm, I thought. Hugh's business partner is banging on his trunk and he fills up like it's nothing. Something really wrong with this picture.

"Do we know how much gas was in the car?" I asked.

"Excuse me?" Antonio said.

"I'm wondering," I said as the Hugh on screen got back into his car and drove out of the shot, "if we know how much gas he bought. Unless he was on empty, why would he stop on the way out there?"

"Ashley, do we have that information?" Antonio asked.

She typed into her iPad for a second. "Doesn't look like it."

"Let's get that then," Bobby said, nodding for Antonio to continue.

"The next time we have any account of Hugh Defry is when his neighbor, a Mrs. Young, saw his car at around 2 am. She doesn't sleep well and often sits on her deck, which faces the garage entrance of Mr. Defry's building."

"Could she see Hugh driving? If there was someone else in the car?" I asked.

Antonio shook his head. "No, it was too dark to see who was in the car, but she recognized his license plate; it's apparently a game she plays with herself."

"What about street cameras?" I asked. Blue raised his head off my lap, his collar letting off a light jingle as he turned toward Antonio, apparently also curious about surveillance cameras around the city.

"Ashley is still gathering the footage."

She nodded. "There are cameras all over this city. I'm going through it as fast as I can."

I nodded. Having spent several years working in London I knew about cities honey combed with cameras.

"How long?" Mulberry asked, turning his body to face Ashley.

"Not sure," she said. "A few more days I'd think, I'm still gathering the footage."

"Let us know if you need another set of eyes," Mulberry said.

"I will," Ashley answered softly. "Thanks." It was almost a purr.

Mulberry turned back to Antonio who continued. "Taggert's body was discovered at approximately 6 am by fishermen." The same photo I'd seen of Taggert's body on the flight appeared on the screen. Taggert's suit jacket spread around him like some kind of water plant, a strange gray lily. Green algae floated on the surface of the water and the shadows glistened black.

"One gunshot to the temple..." A close up of the entry wound, small, cleaned, it looked almost plastic under the medical examiner's harsh lights.

"When officers were dispatched to Mr. Defry's home he answered the door wearing clothing marked with mud and blood. The detectives asked to search the home and garage. Hugh was described as slightly incoherent and nonresistant, offering the officers access."

Edwards cut in. "I think it may be possible to get the whole search thrown out. We've got a tox screen in and should have some answers in a couple of days, but if Hugh was impaired during their search, we may be able to contest consent." He leaned into the center of the table, eyes bright with the challenge.

A photo of the trunk of a car, dark smears marring the beige carpeted interior, filled the screen. "Defry also gave them permission to search his car. The blood found in the trunk matched Taggert's and they found the weapon, a gun,"—its barrel parallel with the edge of a wooden table, lined up against a tape measure flashed on the screen—"on Defry's kitchen table. He has no memory of this gun, the serial number was filed off and ballistics did not match anything in the database...except Mr. Lawrence Taggert's wound."

Resting both hands on the conference table, Edwards rose to his full height and said, "Now that Antonio has told you what we know, let me talk about what we don't know. Here's my first question: What kind of drugs was he on?" He walked around to the front of the table taking the clicker from Antonio who then sat. "We should have the tox screen back by this afternoon. Hopefully it can answer that question for us." He smiled around the room, exuding confidence. "My next question: Who gave the drugs to him? And was that person there?" Edwards pointed at the screen where a photograph of a blood spattered wall glowed. "Now this says to me, and to our experts, that there was somebody standing right here." He reached out and touched the screen, pointing to a blank section of the wall. Circling his finger around it, he continued, "This, ladies and gentleman, is evidence of a leg." He turned back to us. "A leg that does not belong to our client, Mr. Hugh Defry, nor the victim, Mr. Lawrence Taggert. So," he held his hands out to the side. "Who does it belong to?"

No one thought he expected an answer, and so no one offered one. I'd read about his theory on the flight, Hugh had been drugged. Someone else was there. We just had to find out what Hugh was drugged with and by whom. Then we'd have our solution.

Before Edwards could continue there was a knock on the door. We could see through the glass that it was the secretary holding a tray of bagels. Robert opened the door for her. She smiled at him and stepped forward to place the bagels in the center of the table. Robert nodded to Mulberry and then stepped out into the hall. I watched him go for a moment and then, before Edwards started up again dashed through the door, Blue by my side, the secretary still arranging napkins.

EK

He was only a bit down the hall when I closed the conference room door behind me. Bobby stopped and turned. He smiled when he saw Blue and me. "Can I help?" he asked, raising an eyebrow.

"I thought we should talk," I said.

Both brows rose. "Really?"

"Mulberry says I should give you a chance."

"And you listen to him?"

"Don't you?"

He laughed. "Dinner tonight then?"

I nodded. "Okay, where?"

"How about my place? I've got work drinks in the city after so let's make it early. My driver will pick you up. 5:30?"

"How about a public place?"

"You really want to talk about our business in a public place?" he asked. "I'd be happy to meet in your hotel room." I thought about the two of us in a confined space and agreed to meet him at his house.

"I'll drive myself, though," I said.

"You have a car?"

"I will."

"Let me loan you one."

"That's fine, I'll get myself a car."

"Without a license?"

"There are ways."

"I'll have it delivered." He waved to the secretary at the end of the hall and she hurried over to us. "Ms. Jelson, please arrange for the midnight blue Audi A4 to be delivered to Ms. Rye's hotel by 5 pm."

"Of course, sir," she hurried back to her desk and immediately picked up the phone.

"I'll see you tonight," he said, reaching out a hand and squeezing my shoulder before turning away and walking down the hall. I watched until he rounded the corner for the elevator.

EK

Mulberry took me to a restaurant for breakfast, pointing out that I'd avoided the bagels. We sat outside under a big orange umbrella and ordered coffee and eggs with sausage on the side. Blue settled himself under the table and the waitress, who wore skin tight black shorts and a half top in bright pink with the restaurant's logo across her breasts, brought him a bowl of water and a biscuit. He lapped at the water gratefully and accepted the treat once he'd checked with me it was okay.

Once she'd left, I pointed out to Mulberry he'd picked quite the place for breakfast. "Her outfit is awesome."

He smiled. "That's just the culture down here. Everyone is half naked. See," he said, pointing to a man who rollerbladed by wearing only a small pair of cut-off jean shorts, his hairless chest glistening in the sun as he sped by. "It's equal opportunity," he said. I looked down at my outfit and felt my jeans clinging to my legs. I should buy some linen I thought, letting my mind drift back for a moment to my clothing in India, my sarong and T-shirts, how much I'd enjoyed not wearing clothes most of the time.

The waitress returned with our eggs and we ate in silence for a few moments. Mulberry leaned back with a smile, holding his cup of coffee. "I like it here," he said. "Not a bad place to spend a couple of months, maybe half a year. I'm thinking about an apartment in this neighborhood."

"Yeah, I guess," I said. "Though I'm hoping not to be here that long."

Mulberry smiled and leaned across the table toward me. "Sydney, this is going to take time. The wheels of justice are slow."

I took a bite of my eggs and chewed, watching a man wearing an American flag bandana, leather mini skirt, and pink boa bike by, a stereo bungie-corded to the back of the bike playing something with a Latin beat.

"Then why did I have to race over here?" I said, turning back to Mulberry. "If this is all going to take so much time, if we have to wait for the actual justice system to grind out a solution, why did I have to drop everything and get on a plane with you?"

"I thought you'd want to be here," Mulberry said, his brow creasing. "Robert arranged a private jet for you. I was supposed to tell you the night before but..."

He left the sentence open and I felt my face flush as I remember how few words we'd spoken that night.

Mulberry continued, "We got him out on bail only by some kind of miracle."

I coughed on my coffee. "Miracle? Those seem to show up around Bobby Maxim."

"That's why he's good to have around," Mulberry said quietly. He picked up his napkin and wiped at his face. "The man is impressed by you. He wants to work with you. He's the head of the largest and furthest-reaching private investigation firm on the planet. If you don't want to be a part of something like FGI, what do you want to do?"

I took another bite of my eggs.

Mulberry shrugged. "Seems like there is a little punching-the-gift-horse-in-the-mouth thing going on here."

"What?" I asked, angry.

"Don't go all postal on me, Sydney. All I'm saying is you've got an unreasonable dislike for the man."

"He tried to kill me," I said, slamming my fist down. It hit the spoon in the salsa flipping a couple of chunks onto me. "Crap," I said and went to grab my napkin, inadvertently dumping the rest of the container onto my lap. "Shit," I said, jumping up.

The waitress hurried over. "Think you could make more of scene?" Mulberry asked with a sly smile on his face that made my palm itch to wipe it off. I took the extra napkins from the waitress and thanked her. She smiled at Mulberry and I didn't like the look in her eye.

I sat back down, pushing my eggs around with my fork.

Mulberry leaned across the table to me. "Look, Sydney. All I'm saying is don't let your personal feelings fuck this up for Hugh." I felt an *again* at the end of the sentence and resented it.

"I'm having dinner with Robert tonight," I said. "At his house."

Mulberry cocked his head. "Really?"

I shrugged. "You said I should give him a chance."

He frowned but didn't say anything.

"What?"

Mulberry sat back in his chair. He waved for the check and turned back to me. "I had hoped to take you to dinner. Maybe tomorrow night?"

"Did you just ask me out on a date?" I asked, laughing a little at the end.

Mulberry smiled, his cheeks brightening. Jesus Christ, was he blushing? "Yes," he answered.

"No!" I blurted out.

"Jeez, Syd," he said, looking away from me. "That kind of reaction is not good for the ego." When he turned back to me he was smiling, his eyes bright. He leaned across the table looking down at my stained outfit. "You probably need to go shopping," he said.

I looked down at the ruined silk top and thought back to the contents of my bag: jogging clothes, a couple of sundresses, a ratty pair of jeans, an extra bra, my leather jacket, a T-shirt with a rip in one armpit, and two white T-shirts, both with stains. I looked down at my one good outfit. The jeans were salvageable. "I wanted to go see *Defry's*," I said.

"I'll drop you there. Lincoln Road is nearby, you can get whatever you need there."

CHAPTER FIVE
DANGEROUS DRESS SHOPPING

Blue and I stood in front of the restaurant after Mulberry drove away. It had a green awning with Hugh's last name, *Defry*, scrawled across it in white. The space for outdoor seating was empty, a gap in the sidewalk. The windows were dark.

A couple approached, both dressed in beachwear, their skin glistening with sunscreen. They stopped in front of the restaurant a couple of paces from me.

"That was the restaurant from that show, right?," said the woman to the man.

"Yeah," he answered.

"So sad," she said.

"Do you think it was for ratings?" he asked.

She slapped his arm. "That's terrible."

He smiled down at her and they began to walk again. Never glancing at Blue or me, as if we were invisible. I didn't even want them to consciously not look at me. Just let their brains filter me out. Keep the world the way it was supposed to be. Hugh was the one who told me how to hide. As long as you were something most people didn't want to see they wouldn't.

I wondered if Hugh knew that being that unwanted *thing* meant you'd stepped behind a curtain. That you were back there with all of your own kind. That as much as you hid, you were also drawn. Did Hugh know this because he was a killer, too?

Back in New York, when I realized that the bullet I'd just shot thunked into a corpse instead of the living, breathing man who killed my brother, I hardly had time to think. His security burst through the doors and I ran for my life. When I found out it was Bobby Maxim who stole my revenge, I blamed him for everything. The death of my brother, my own failure to avenge him, for the creature I felt myself becoming.

But I didn't try to kill Bobby. I held back, not wanting to do the exact thing that he expected of me. When Robert offered an end to Joy Humbolt in exchange for tracking down his Mexican friend's missing daughter I went along, hoping to put my past behind me. But the girl, Ana Maria Hernandez Vargas, turned out to be a manipulative, cold-blooded killer who screwed me six ways from Sunday. Right as I was exacting my revenge on her, exposing the rat that she was, Robert sent stupid men with lots of guns after me and my friends, including fucking Mulberry. In the end, Robert disposed of Ana Maria more permanently than I planned. He also killed Joy Humbolt. Her body was found, her case closed, the manhunt ended, and I was free to be Sydney Rye. So, again, I didn't try to kill him.

But here's the fucked up thing. While I didn't kill Bobby Maxim, I killed a shit ton of other people in my time as Sydney Rye. A shit ton of men, to be more specific. Guys who took advantage of their strength and cruelty to subjugate others. But more important than any moral ground I thought I stood on was the hole in the pit of my stomach, the unfulfilled promise that made me want to tear everything apart. Did Hugh have the same hole? No, I thought turning away from the restaurant and heading down the street. Hugh was innocent and I was going to prove it. But first, I needed some clothing.

EK

Lincoln Road ran east to west away from the beach toward the bay. It was like an outdoor mall with a wide plaza between the stores where restaurants had seating and street performers entertained for tips. Waiters and waitresses were setting the tables in the center. They hurried from inside the restaurants out into the sun, carrying cutlery wrapped in napkins, plates, and glasses. There were few pedestrians at this hour but the place buzzed with the anticipation of the lunch crowd.

Between the restaurants were clothing and accessories stores, their brightly lit windows filled with proposed outfits. Doors propped open letting the air conditioning float out. Looking at the displays, I tried to imagine myself in a pair of straight leg jeans, a button-down shirt, and a fitted blazer but it seemed so wholly ridiculous. Blue and I wandered in and out of the shops, working our way lazily down the street, my mind mulling and turning.

A gold flash flickered at the corner of my eye, and I turned to see a darkened store front. Except one of the mannequins was wearing a gold sequined dress that caught the sun in a brilliant display of twinkles. I walked over to it. The dress was strapless and short, not the kind of thing you could bend over in. Too short even for a knife on the inner thigh. But with that much leg you could probably keep a small pistol between…my eyes shifted focus and I saw a group of people standing in the store.

It was dark inside. I flicked my eyes to the closed sign on the front door, then back to the group. Three women, thin, drawn, frightened, dressed provocatively like the mannequins in the window. And two men, thick brows and flattened noses, short hair, eyes that told me to fuck off. Blue nuzzled my hip. I decided to try the door.

It was mirrored, reflecting the plaza behind me, the growing lunch crowd, a man setting up to play an accordion, the sun a bright globe of light almost at its apex. I tested the handle, pulling slightly, not locked. A small panel listed the store hours. They were supposed to be open.

I was sure the group inside could see me. So I yanked hard, jumping out of the way . The sun shot through in a blinding ray. I stepped into the beam, backlit. The men squinted at me, their pupils little pin pricks. The women shielded their eyes, holding up forearms against the light. There were finger bruises on the pale flesh of one girl. Ligature marks, fading but still visible, on the wrists of the other two. Blue's and my shadow stopped five feet in front of the cluster.

"We're closed," the bigger of the two men yelled, his accent Slavic. He was a little closer to me, to the left of the girls who stood between the men. He wore a pair of jeans with an Eastern European cut and faux wear on the knees and thighs. The smaller guy was balding, his head shaved. He wore a tight black T-shirt that showed off a defined chest and strong shoulders. Tattoos started at his wrists and wound up his arms, Cyrillic lettering interspersed with swastikas was the theme. Oh, and titties.

When I didn't respond to the big guy's question the smaller one smirked. "What are you, blind and deaf?" he asked, his accent thicker. It took me a second to realize he thought I was blind and that Blue was my seeing eye dog.

The door began to swing shut behind me, sweeping darkness across the floor. It closed with a soft click.

"Get out," the big one told me again. He was starting to look angry, his shoulders bunching up, making his neck look comically short.

"Do you speak English?" I asked the women. The one with the forearm bruises understood me, I could see it in her eyes. But she didn't answer.

"You go now, we are closed," the big one said.

"Are you okay?" I asked her.

He started toward me. The woman licked her lips and then pulled the bottom one between her teeth, biting down on it. She had big brown eyes and stringy blonde hair that hung down to her bony shoulders. She was wearing a bright blue dress. Its rich color made her pale skin look gray. The smaller man reached out and grabbed her bicep, shaking her hard. She winced and lowered her eyes to the ground, teetering on high heels.

Blue growled and raised his hackles. The big man's approach stuttered but didn't stop. He reached out, as if to take my left arm. Blue's growl grew louder. The man's fingers touched my skin. I squatted low twisting my body away from him and fisting my right hand. Blue barked, high pitched and grating, throwing the big guy off as much as my quick movement. Pushing into the ground, I rocketed my body up, extending my right arm while keeping a slight bend in the elbow, and plowed into the guy's chin.

He stumbled back, his neck exposed. Pivoting fast I drove my left fist into his throat. His hands flew up, clutching at his neck. The man's feet lost contact with the ground, his knees buckled, and he landed on his ass hard enough that I felt it through the floor. Staring up at me with bulging eyes he coughed on a breath. Wheezed and coughed again.

I looked up and the smaller man was struggling to pull a gun out of his pants while still clutching onto the girl. She was shaking violently and pulling away from him, the whites of her eyes visible in her panic. The sight of his pistol had snagged in his pants, and all he needed to do was let go of the girl and free it, but he was too shocked, his body wouldn't let him release her. And that was going to cost him.

Blue leapt forward, placing his front paws on the big guy's shoulders, knocking him flat on his back. I knew he'd placed his teeth against the man's already bruised throat but I didn't wait to watch. I ran as fast as I could toward the guy with the grip. His eyes widened in the moment it took me to close the space between us and his gun arm pulled harder.

Pivoting sideways I used my momentum to jam my elbow into his solar plexus, keeping it there as he bent around my arm, his face almost touching my shoulder. He let go of the girl and she fell back with a small cry. Straightening my arm, I reached down and wrapped my hand around his, sneaking my finger in front of his and over the trigger. With my free hand I grabbed him behind the neck. He went very still. Our faces were a breath away from each other, his chin pressed on the back of my bicep, body curled around the gun aimed at his junk.

Sweat poured down his brow and his mouth was open, sucking in air. The man's heartbeat thumped in his chest, and I could feel it against my arm. He was very much alive and knew that could be extremely temporary.

Blue's low growl permeated the air and I could hear the big man's wheezing breaths. Quieter still was the soft mewls of the women, they were good at crying silently. "I know you can understand me," I said to the woman, while keeping my eyes on the man.

Her friends had helped her up and now they stood together, a tight huddle, backs against the wall, the one in blue slightly in front of the other two. Their long exposed legs teetering on high heels made them look like a tightly knit group of trees shaking in the wind.

"We've got a situation here," I said to the man. He blinked. "What do you suggest we do?"

His brow furrowed slightly, his breath was returning to normal. "Let go?" When he spoke his chin pressed deeper into my muscle.

I smiled. "Unbutton your pants."

"Fuck off," he said.

"Should I have my dog kill your friend?"

His mouth twitched up, he was feeling a little confident that his dick might make it through. For all I knew the safety was on. For all I knew, if I pressed his finger harder, nothing would happen. But as soon as I applied pressure his mouth puckered and he twitched his hip back. "Unbutton your pants."

He reached around and pulled, the jeans unsnapped and loosened, freeing the gun. The idiot grabbed for it, pulling the muzzle down, pushing my finger into his, and his into the trigger. The bang sounded real loud that close up. I felt hot blood explode over my hand and up my arm. His fingers went limp, eyes rolled into the back of his head, and the man slid down my arm then fell sideways onto the ground, his hand still stuck under mine. Blood and chunks of flesh covered our joining, and sizzled on the tip of the hot gun barrel. The smell of burned flesh filled the air.

I dropped the gun, his arm flopped to the ground. Then I kicked it away from him, sending it skittering under a rack of clothes leaving a splatter of blood in its wake. "Lock the door," I said to the girl. She didn't move for a second. "Please," I said, and caught her eyes, filling mine with goodwill and strength. She stepped toward me and then scurried past the smaller man, giving the big guy, still under Blue's control, a wide berth. She reached the door and turned the dead bolt.

I grabbed a dress off the rack and wiped off my hand and arm as best I could, throwing the garment onto the floor when done. My shirt was officially ruined. Pulling out my phone I called Malina, one of the first people to know me as Sydney Rye. She owed me a lot and always picked up when I called. "Sydney," she said, and I could practically see the grin, full lips drawn wide over perfect white teeth. In the background I heard a man's voice squawking over a loudspeaker and the sounds of a crowd.

"Do you know anyone in Miami?" I asked.

Her voice dropped low and serious. "Sydney. What's happening?"

"I need someone with connections in your world, and I need that person now. Do you have anyone you trust?"

"Yes."

EK

Less than three minutes later my phone rang. It was a local number. I answered. "Malina said you needed help. I am at your disposal," said a male voice, rich and foreign. His accent sounded African, I thought. Senegalese maybe. Dead sexy, definitely.

I told him my situation. While waiting for his call I'd gagged, blindfolded, and tied up the big guy in a back office I found. The other one was still breathing but leaking blood at a pace that wouldn't last. He remained unconscious, but I'd bound his hands just in case. The women stood together, watching me and whispering quietly to each other. They were no longer shaking. When I finished my account the man said, "I am on my way. You should leave."

"What? I'm not just leaving them here."

"Go out the back door. You will come to an alley. The third door to your right will bring you into the back room of a salon. You can leave through the shop."

"But-"

"If you want my help you will do as I say." I didn't answer right away. "You have no choice but to trust me. Now go." He hung up the phone.

I looked over at the three women. "Someone is on his way," I said. "He's going to take you to safety."

The woman in blue stared at me then spoke for the first time. "Who are you?" she asked, her voice unsure but the accent pretty good. I could still hear a hint of her native tongue. She came from somewhere cold and harsh with a language that matched its dark and dangerous landscape.

"Safe travels," I said and then followed Malina's friend's advice, entering the alley and running a couple of doors down to the salon. The door was unlocked and I stepped into an air-conditioned room. The three sinks with seats backing up to them made it clear this space was used for hair washing. Right by the door was a shelving unit filled with dyes, shampoos, and other supplies.

I grabbed a smock off a shelf and quickly threw it around myself, snapping the buttons at the base of my neck. Blue sat slightly behind me, head low, scrunching into himself, trying to look smaller. The door opened and a woman walked in. She startled when she saw me, then placed her hand over her heart and smiled. "I am sorry, you gave me a start. I didn't know you were back here." She held her hand out pointing toward the row of sinks. "I'm Missy, let me get you shampooed. Who are you here to see?" she asked.

I smiled. "I'm not sure of their name," I said. "My hotel made the arrangements and I just walked over." I sat in the chair, being careful to keep my hands under the fabric. Blue sat next to me. The woman walked around me glancing at Blue. "Nice dog," she said.

"Thanks, it's great you're pet friendly."

"Sure," she said. I heard her turn the tap, the rush of water from the spout.

"What are you thinking of having done?" she asked, pressing on my shoulder for me to lean back.

I slid into the seat, my neck resting on the cool porcelain. "Something drastic," I answered.

EK

When I got back to my suite I kicked off my shoes and unbuttoned the smock from around my neck. I'd convinced the hairdresser I loved it and wanted to keep it. She told me it did look nice. Her face didn't agree with her words but she went along with it.

I unbuttoned my stained shirt and, grabbing a plastic laundry bag from the closet, pushed it in. Peeling off my jeans I dropped them into the bag and then tied it off. I took a shower and scrubbed at my skin. I'd taken a trip to the ladies room at the salon and gotten as much off my hand and arm as I could, but it had soaked through my shirt and onto my stomach and ribs. After the shower I climbed into bed. Blue jumped up and settled at my feet, his chin resting on my calf. I dialed Malina's number. She picked up.

"Is everything okay?" I asked.

"Perfect, Sydney, everything is perfect."

"Good," I said, feeling the exhaustion of relief and jet lag come at me.

"You sound tired, Sydney. Is everything all right?"

"Hugh is in real trouble, Malina," I said.

"Dan told me."

I bit my lip feeling a surge of emotion. "I'm exhausted.'

"Take a nap. You will feel better."

My last thought before sleep descended on me like a heavy blanket, was that, so far, I'd been pretty useless to Hugh.

I woke to someone knocking at the door. Blue rushed out of the bedroom and through the living room toward the entrance. I followed, pausing to grab a robe from the bathroom. When I checked the peep hole I saw a bellboy, resplendent in his tasseled uniform. I need to switch hotels, I thought, before opening the door.

"Ms. Sydney Rye?" he asked.

"Yes?"

"This came for you," he said, holding up a large white box with a skull and cross bones patterned ribbon tied around it.

"Oh," I said, taken aback. He passed it to me and I put it inside the room. "Who delivered it?" I asked, as I grabbed my purse off the entrance table and pulled out a $20 bill.

"Don't know, Miss. Sorry," he said, eyeing the bill in my hand. I thanked him, handing over the money.

Back in my room I placed the box on the bed. I looked for a card but there was just the large and floppy satin bow. I pulled on it, the knot falling out of place easily. Inside, a handwritten note sat on top of folded black tissue paper.

I thought you might have nothing to wear, what with your tiny duffle. Looking forward to this evening.

-Robert

I pulled back the paper under which was a dress. Black and ruched it lay nestled in the tissue. I thought back to the last time I'd been given a dress. It was in New York. The man who gave it to me later fucked my brains out in a way I found downright delicious. It was the same night I met Bobby Maxim.

I wasn't afraid when I went to that party in a dress given to me by my lover. I was excited. Exhilarated. Was this how Bobby still thought of me? As Joy Humbolt, unafraid, playing with the idea of being naughty.

I lifted it up. Unfurled, the dress proved to be about knee length with cap sleeves and a sweetheart neckline. Dropping it back on the bed, I untied my robe and threw it on the spare bed. Picking up Robert's dress I held it in front of myself using the full length mirror on the back of the closet to judge my appearance.

The ruched material caught the light here and there, reflecting almost silver against the black. It made my eyes flash. I put it on, pushing the material down my hips. It fit like a fine glove, hugging every curve. However, the rough texture, cap sleeves, and ladylike length made it elegant. I turned, checking my back--the dress covered my shoulder blades. The material hugged my ass, following its curve around, but not so far that it became obscene.

In this dress I could strap a knife to my thigh. I pulled up the hem. It came easily, as the material was made to scrunch. My phone rang and I dropped the dress, feeling almost guilty.

The screen showed a picture of Dan, smiling against a setting sun, sitting on our veranda in Goa. I bit my lip feeling an ache of regret and loss. The last time we'd spoken I'd been at a private airport in Delhi, huddled into a quiet corner, my cellphone pressed to my cheek, a glass of seltzer bubbling on the table next to me. Mulberry sat at the bar, his eyes trained on the TV but his tight shoulders and clenching jaw made it clear his attention was on me. Our flight out of India left in 30 minutes.

I was in Delhi and Dan was in Paris. I'd asked him to go, to take our friend, Anita, to safety. And I had to tell him, over the phone across all those miles, that I slept with Mulberry. My voice was low and I felt queazy. I cut off my thoughts and picked up the phone.

"Hey," I said.

"Sydney," I could sense a smile on his lips. "How are you?"

"Fine," I said.

"How's Hugh?"

"In trouble."

"I'm in Miami." I felt a thrill run through me. "I want to help." I wet my lips but didn't respond. Dan continued. "I'm not asking for anything but to help. Can I come over, so we can at least talk? Our last conversation was so brief."

"You hung up on me."

I heard him laugh low in his throat. "If the situation were reversed what would you have done?"

"Dan...I."

"We need to talk," Dan said, his voice forceful.

I looked at the clock. There was still time before I needed to leave for Robert's. I told Dan which hotel I was in.

"I'm at the airport," he said. "I'll be there soon."

I hung up the phone and saw my reflection in the mirror staring back at me. My hair, now bleached blonde, the bangs and sides framing my face in a tight rectangle, looked almost like a warrior's helmet. The tight black dress hugged every dangerous curve. I felt fierce. Not at all like someone you should love or trust with their heart.

Before I'd slept with Mulberry, left India, taken my whole life and my two closest relationships and smashed them together littering pieces of lust and hurt all over the damn place, Dan had asked me to join him. To use the network of Joyful Justice to create our own organization. To help people, make a difference, fight for the little guy, all the cheesy shit an organization called Joyful Justice might be into. The only promise I'd ever made Dan was to think about his offer and instead I'd run from it as fast and as far as I could. I owed him an answer. I owed myself an answer.

Staring into my own eyes I thought of Mulberry's question: If I didn't want to work with an organization like FGI then what did I want to do?

Blue came and sat next to me, he leaned against my leg and pushed at my stomach with his muzzle, asking for pets. Looking down at him, I smiled and rubbed under his chin. "What do you think?" I asked. His ears perked. "What should we do?"

He didn't have an answer for me.

I decided to wear the dress. Why not let Robert Maxim keep his ideas of me? This evening was about me getting inside his head, not the other way around. Besides, I hadn't actually gotten any shopping done.

I found my garter knife sheath in my duffel and pulled it over my foot and up my leg, positioning it inside my thigh within easy reach from the front or back. I pushed the small knife into the holster feeling calmer with its hilt pressing against my flesh.

The phone rang, and when I answered, a polite female voice announced Dan was downstairs. I gave my permission for him to come up and then, still barefoot, checked my reflection again, running my fingers through my hair. I opened the door and looked down the hall. Empty. Blue pushed his head into my hand and sat next to me, leaning against my thigh and turning his head to follow my gaze to the elevators.

A ding announced the lift's arrival and Dan stepped out. He looked away from me first and I licked my lips, biting down on the bottom one, taking the moment to watch him. He wore loose jeans with a striped linen shirt I remembered buying with him in Mumbai months ago. It was always a favorite of mine, the subtle green stripes bringing out the shades in his eyes.

Blue's ears perked, and as Dan turned toward us, I looked down at him and nodded. He took off down the hall, tail wagging, letting out a bark of excitement. Dan's face broke into a grin. "Hey boy," he said as Blue reached him, skidding to a stop. He lowered his head and lifted his tail, hopping from side to side with excitement. Dan patted his thigh and Blue quickly took position next to him pushing his nose against

Dan's hip. Dan pet him, rubbing his muzzle and ear as they walked toward me.

"Hey," he said to me and wrapped his free arm around my waist, pulling me into a hug. I fell against him, reaching up both arms and encircling his neck. He was warm and smelled like himself. It took all my strength not to run my nose against the exposed skin of his neck, breathing him in. "I like the new hair," he said. "Very Miami."

I pulled away and he looked down at my dress and cocked his head. "I have dinner plans," I said. His jaw clenched. "I need to leave in about a half hour," I added. He nodded, not looking me in the eye. "Please come in," I said, pushing the door wider.

He passed me, stepping into the room and crossing to the windows. "Nice view," he said.

"Thanks." I looked past him to the ocean and sky, colored in the soft tones of dusk. "How's Anita?" I asked. The last time I'd seen Dan he was headed to the airport with Anita, who'd been brutally beaten and just committed her first murder, in self defense, of course.

"Good," he said, not turning around. "She's got a new project she's working on. I think it's really helping her."

"Project?" I asked. Anita was a reporter, a damn good one. She owed me enough that I figured she would keep her promise never to write about me, but...

"Who's dinner with?" Dan asked, still facing the ocean.

"Robert Maxim."

His shoulders tensed and he snorted a laugh.

"What?" I asked.

"You don't want me to answer that," he said, keeping his back turned.

"No, really, what?" I said.

"As I recall when we first met, he was your enemy and Mulberry was suspect. Now you've fallen into bed with one and are dining with the other."

My face felt hot. "You make it sound so simple." He turned back into the room, the ocean glinting behind him. I took a deep breath. "Hugh is in trouble, and I'm trying to help. I thought that's what you wanted, too."

Backlit by the last light of the day, it was hard to see Dan's face. "You're right," he said, his voice sounding calm again. "That is what I want."

"Do you think that's a good idea?"

"You don't trust me." He took a step toward me.

"I don't trust me," I said, feeling a pull toward him.

"I just, I really want-"

A knock on the door interrupted us as Dan reached for me. I turned to look at the entrance. Blue ran to the door, barked, and sat. Mulberry, I thought, and then Dan's hand was in my hair. He turned my head capturing me in a kiss. His other arm wrapped around my waist and pulled me against him. Without thinking I responded, burying my fingers in his hair, my leg bending up to curl around him, pressing the hilt of the knife into the sensitive flesh of my inner thigh.

Blue barked again and I pulled away, my breathing heavy. Dan looked down at me, his eyes roaming my face. I disentangled from him and straightened my skirt as I walked over to the door. Checking the peep hole my suspicion was proven right; Mulberry waited in the hall.

I sighed involuntarily and opened the door feeling Dan's kiss on my lips and the wild beating of my heart against my breast. Mulberry smiled nervously and immediately began talking. "Hey, sorry to bother you, I know you're leaving soon but I just wanted to talk to you before you left. Can I come in?"

Dan walked up behind me. "Mulberry," he said, his voice cold.

Mulberry's nervousness disappeared and he stood up tall, straightening his broad shoulders. "Dan, I didn't know you were here."

"I only just arrived."

"Don't worry," I said to Mulberry, trying to end this as quickly as possible. "I'm not planning anything stupid for tonight."

"What's going on?" Dan asked.

The ding of the elevator was quickly followed by the sound of children's voices headed our way.

"Let me in," Mulberry said, making eye contact.

"Fine," I said, stepping aside for him to enter. For a moment Dan blocked his path and the two men stared at each other, the air between them pulsing. Blue pushed up against Dan's hand and he turned back into the room, Mulberry following behind him.

Seeing the dress box where I'd left it on the couch, Mulberry walked over to it and picked up the note. He turned to me. "Robert sent you that dress?"

"Yes," I answered, raising my chin.

Mulberry ran his hand through his hair and licked his lips. "Do you think you should wear it? Didn't you go shopping today?"

"Why wouldn't I wear it?" I asked, ignoring the second part of that question. "You said I could trust him."

"What's going on?" Dan asked.

"Mulberry told me to trust Robert Maxim despite the fact that every cell in my being tells me he set this whole thing up to get me here."

"I don't think he is going to hurt you," Mulberry said, his voice louder than it needed to be. His eyes whipped to Dan and then back to me. "But, he, I wouldn't be surprised if he came on to you. Hard."

"So I should trust him, but not *too* much," I said anger building in my chest at both of them being there at all, at Bobby Maxim for being who he was, at myself for not knowing what to do, for the burning lips and the heat I felt. "You don't think I can resist him?" I asked. "Am I so easy?"

Mulberry's eyes darkened. My eyes narrowed as I stared back at him. Flicking my eyes to Dan I saw him staring at the ground. Neither of them answered me. Blue's nose nudged my hip, reminding me he was there.

I took a step back. My lip curled. "Fuck both of you," I said my voice low. Neither of them looked at me. "I never promised either of you anything, but you still think you own me."

"It's just—" Dan started and then gave up.

"It's just what, Dan?" I shook my head. "If I'm such a slut, how come you're both so in love with me?" Their eyes jumped to my face. It was almost like I'd slapped them. "Get out," I said, feeling the rage building inside me. "Now," I said. Blue growled low in his throat, backing me up.

CHAPTER SIX
A FUCK OR A FIGHT

When I got downstairs I was still fuming. I crossed through the lobby, my mind filled—the look on Dan and Mulberry's faces, the thumping of my heart, the heat in my chest. So when a bellboy touched my elbow, I whirled around on him quickly and aggressively. Blue let out a low growl and the young man stumbled back. It was the same kid who delivered the dress and I took a deep breath before apologizing.

He smiled nervously. "Mr. Maxim asked me to give you this." He held up a key fob with the Audi symbol on it. "Your car is waiting outside."

"Thank you," I said, taking the fob from him. In the hotel's half moon drive, a midnight blue Audi A4 was the only car without a driver. It was parked in a tow zone. I crossed to it and stood for a moment. Its headlights reminded me of panther eyes. I felt a thrill and realized that this was going to be fun.

Blue's head grazed the ceiling of the passenger side. I pulled out onto Ocean Drive and followed the instructions programmed into the car's navigation system. The traffic was slow, this was a street more for showing off than getting somewhere. Eyes drifted across the car, taking in the dark metal, the sculpted lines, the Audi symbol that told everyone how much this beast cost. People crowded the streets, girls in short skirts and high heels, men with broad shoulders and recently cut hair.

They all looked good, in their best outfits, out to find a fuck or a fight. The same as a million others who roamed the streets of any city in any part of the world. It often amazed me how different we all were and yet how still the same instincts drew us from our homes and out into the night.

As we inched along, Blue let out a yelp and I turned to see Dan and Mulberry standing next to a beat up Land Cruiser parked in an alley off the main drag. Mulberry ran a hand through his hair and looked at the ground. Dan shook his head and opened up the door of the SUV and said one more thing before climbing in. It must be his car, I thought. It occurred to me that Dan had lived in Key West before I'd called him away. He'd never mentioned what kind of car he drove and I'd never asked. Mulberry turned away and walked deeper into the shadowed alley as Dan's car turned on, the brake lights glowing. A car tooted behind me and I realized the light was green.

We reached the highway, and when I opened Blue's window he stuck his nose out so that as we picked up speed his ears flapped in the wind and he half closed his eyes, letting the long lashes touch to protect his sensitive irises from the rushing wind. I barely began to feel the power of my new ride when the GPS told me to turn onto Star Island. I slowed and made the right, crossing a bridge to where a guard booth waited, a long arm blocking the road any further.

I rolled down my window as a smiling guard asked my intentions. "I'm here to see Robert Maxim," I said. He nodded and let me through. I would have thought he'd needed my name or some kind of ID. As I passed under the gate I saw before me a long, narrow park that ran through the center of the island. It formed an oval with the road ringed around it. The name of the park was displayed on a sign installed by the city. They weren't really allowed to keep people off this island, I thought, as I drove along the park, they just liked to pretend they did. A guard booth was certainly enough to dissuade unsure oglers from crossing the bridge.

To my right, opposite the park, were walls covered in tropical vegetation. A dense mix of green vines, bushes bursting with bright flowers, and wide fronds waving gently in the breeze was periodically interrupted by gates marking the different homes. Each had its own flair, Brass Lions here, entwined Dolphins there. The GPS directed me to Robert's. His gate was solid, oxidized steel. There was nothing to see but a speaker box and the impenetrable metal.

I pulled up to the intercom and rolled down my window. Blue leaned across me, his nose pulsing, hoping to see if my side of the car revealed any new scents. Before I had a chance to speak, the gate began to open. Looking up, I saw a small camera mounted in a nearby tree. Of course, he was waiting for me. Or at least someone was.

The receding gate revealed a driveway leading to a house, white and large. As I approached, I saw it was a classic from the twenties that had been updated by just the right modern architect. The result was something at once grand and modern, maintaining the stateliness of the original home. There was nothing gaudy or ugly about it.

I took a deep breath as I pulled up to the entrance. The driver, Claude, hurried down the steps and opened my door for me as I turned off the car. Blue followed me out and Claude led us up the stairs and into the house.

EK

We passed through a grand entrance way and down a short hall. Claude showed me into a large and airy living room, one wall of which was glass panels. This mild evening they were pushed to the side letting in a cool breeze that ruffled the surface of an unlit infinity pool that flowed right into the house, bringing the salty scent of the sea and the sweetness of night jasmine with it. Across the bay, the glass high-rises of Miami reflected the deep blue of the sky. Their lights twinkled brighter each moment as the sun slipped further beneath the horizon.

Claude closed the door behind me, and I stood for a moment surveying the room from a marble landing. Four steps down brought us to the living room where two leather chairs and a deep gray canvas couch faced the view. A grand piano was placed to the side, its top covered in photographs. A bar curled along one wall, shelves lined with bottles lit from behind.

It was masculine without being chauvinistic. The interior designer had done a good job. I walked over to the piano taking a closer look at the photographs. Blue sat by my side, letting his shoulder brush against my leg. Bobby Maxim was in most of the pictures. In two of them, he was shaking hands with former presidents. Another showed him, younger, wearing a suit with lapels only appropriate to the 80s with his arm around a starlet I recognized as famous but couldn't place. The oldest photograph showed Bobby, his face soft and boyish, standing between an older man and woman I assumed to be his parents. Bobby smiled out at the camera wearing a cap and gown, his mother and father looked proud as they squinted against the day's bright sun. They were both shorter than him and dressed in Sunday best that wasn't that great.

Blue let out a low growl, and then I heard the the door open. Turning around I saw Robert Maxim, the man himself, standing at the top of the landing. He smiled and his gaze glided over me. I suddenly felt the fabric of the dress tight across my stomach, hugging my thighs, pushing at my breasts.

"You look wonderful," he said as he came down the steps. "The dress fits you perfectly, I'm very pleased." His suit was charcoal and cut to show off his shoulders and tapered waist. Open at the neck, his white shirt contrasted with his tan skin. A pocket square completed the debonair look.

"Yes," I said, glancing down at myself. "At first I thought it was far too extravagant a gift but then, I figured, you owed me." He laughed. "Whoever picked it out did a good job."

He frowned. "I picked it out." Close now, he looked down at me. "When I bought it I wondered where you'd hide your weapon. I know you've got one on you." He licked his lips. "I'd love the chance to find it."

I laughed. "You are such a cliché."

He smiled. "Cliché?"

"Rich guy like you, multiple wives, hits on employees—"

"Ah, so you're agreeing to be my employee?"

"No."

"Well, you're the only one I hit on."

I laughed. "Yeah, right. And I bet you're an excellent piano player.

That's why you keep it in your living room. It's not just a prop for pictures of you with famous people?"

He grinned and took a seat on the bench. Flipping up the lid, he laid his elegant fingers to the keys, then looked up at me and began to play. A soft trill followed by another, his hands leapt up and then came down quickly, like jumping spiders, and he was off, fingers flying across the keys, then slowing and gently teasing, the pace picked up again and, as he bent over the piano, a lock of his hair fell against his forehead and danced with each movement. As the song came to a close he looked up at me again and smiled. His fingers slipped to his sides and he turned away from the keys. Standing, he said, "It was my mother's. She played every day."

"Do you?"

He shrugged. "Not as much as she'd like."

"You sounded good."

"I believe that's the first time you've ever complimented me."

I shrugged and looked over at the bar. "Aren't you going to offer a lady a drink?"

He laughed. "Of course." We crossed the room together, Blue staying between us, and then Robert stepped behind the bar. "What can I get you? Wine, whiskey, tequila gimlet?"

"You've done your homework." He smiled and turned to grab a bottle of tequila from the shelf. As he mixed my tequila gimlet I looked around the room again. "How's Pammy and Toby?" I asked after his wife and dog. I'd first met Maxim when I became his dog walker back in New York City. So, you could say I met him through his dog.

"Toby hasn't been the same since you left. The new dog walker's a real pill," he said turning back to me, gently shaking my cocktail. Pulling a chilled glass from under the counter he placed it on the bar in front of me. "Pam and I divorced last year," he smiled. "We share custody of Toby."

I laughed as he poured the shimmering pale red liquid into a martini glass. "Really? I never got the sense you loved that dog."

Bobby looked up at me as he shook the final drops into my glass. He shrugged with one shoulder.

"Your third wife?"

"Yes."

"Last?"

"You never know," he said pushing the glass over to me. I sipped off the top millimeter.

"Probably for the best, the divorce, I mean. Pammy and Bobby, you always did sound like a prom queen and king from the 50s."

He laughed. "I, my dear, graduated high school in the 70s."

I shrugged and sipped my drink.

Leaning his elbows on the bar and bringing his face closer to mine he continued, "You would have loved the 70s."

"Oh really?"

"Yes, they were wild. Everything went."

"And that's what you think I'm into?"

"I know it is." He leaned back and reaching under the counter pulled out a bottle of Bourbon. "Seems unfair doesn't it?" he asked.

"What?"

"That men can do whatever they want, sexually, and be considered masculine but a woman does anything to impinge her reputation, and she's a slut."

I raised my eyebrows wondering if he had my room bugged. "All those wives and lovers but no children?" I asked, changing the subject.

He shook his head. "You're getting personal this evening," he said while he filled a crystal tumbler with ice.

"I'm trying to understand you. Mulberry says I should give you a chance."

"He's right."

"Really," I leaned on the bar and twirled the stem of my glass. "What about you trying to kill me and my friends? Did they have orders to kill Blue as well?"

I looked up at him and he paused from pouring whiskey over ice. "I was very angry," he said and when he looked up from the glass there was a flash in his eyes, a hint of that rage still bubbling beneath. "I realize now it was misplaced. You had not betrayed me."

When I didn't respond he put down the bottle and continued. "I am rarely fooled. I didn't like the feeling. I'm sorry."

I thought about how I'd fallen for Ana Maria's bullshit, too. I hadn't liked the feeling but I didn't try to kill her. Robert did. And, honestly, I didn't mind. "What would you have done?" he asked quietly. "I thought you'd killed my friends and kidnapped their child."

I sipped my drink. "And now you want what from me?"

A bell rang and Bobby looked up. "Dinner is ready," he said.

The dining room was formal with high backed chairs, a long rectangular table, candles flickering down its center. There were two places set, one at the head and one to its right. Bobby pulled my chair out for me and, as I sat, he pushed it in. Blue went under the table and laid down, resting his chin on my foot. Bobby sat at the head of the table. A maid came in, dressed for the part in a knee length powder blue uniform and apron. Her black hair, streaked with gray, was pulled back into a tight bun and she smiled at me as she placed my tequila gimlet by my side. After bringing Bobby his whiskey, she left the room, closing the door behind her. The walls were cloth I noticed, buffering the sound. "You have a lot of parties in here?" I asked.

Bobby sipped from his drink before answering. "Yes, a fair number. In our business there is quite a bit of entertaining."

"Our business?" I asked. "You think we're in the same business?"

He laughed softly and sat back in his chair. "You really think we are so different? That you're so much more noble than me?" I bit my lip. "I love it when you do that," he said and leaned forward quickly, his movements suddenly animal like. His smooth speed reminded me how careful I needed to be around this man.

"We're not alike," I said, forcing myself not to pull away from him, to meet his eyes.

He smiled slowly, his lips sliding over teeth that gleamed in the soft candlelight. The maid returned and he sat back. She placed salads in front of each of us and then left again. "Would you like to switch to wine?" Bobby asked me.

"No, this is fine." I picked up my drink and sipped, letting the liquor curl around my mouth, and clenched my jaw.

"Have you read Machiavelli?" Bobby asked.

I put down my drink and shook my head. "No, but I know the general theme about means and ends."

"Yes, that the ends justify the means is a tenet of his philosophy, but it is more nuanced than that." He reached into his inside pocket and pulled out a slim paperback book. "I saw this in a used book store the other day and thought of you. I hope you can accept another gift from me." He placed the thin treatise next to my plate. *The Prince* by Machiavelli. I reached out and touched its worn cover but didn't answer. He placed his hand over mine and I quickly withdrew it.

"If you think anything is going to happen between us tonight you're fucking nuts," I said.

He laughed. "God, I love that about you."

"You keep talking about things you love about me and I'm going to leave."

"I'm sorry." He put his hands up in the air. "I'll be better."

"Why don't we just cut the crap and you tell me what it is you want from me. What are your ends, Maxim?"

"I want you to work with me."

"With you, who works with you? Is the lady in the maid uniform working with you or *for* you. I don't work for anyone anymore."

"Sydney, when I first met you all I wanted was to fuck you." He leaned back in his chair, relaxed, the whiskey held lightly in one of his elegant hands. "But as I've gotten to know you, I've come to realize how special you really are."

"You don't know me," I shot back.

He smiled. "Not as well as I'd like to. But well enough that I know I want you on my side. Sydney, I could see you running Fortress Global when I retire."

My jaw dropped.

"Don't look so surprised."

"That is entirely insane."

"Why?"

"I wouldn't run it like you."

"No, what would you do differently?" He smiled and sipped from his whiskey glass, his eyes sparkling in the candlelight. "You can't hide from me and why would you want to? I like what I see, all of it."

I shook my head. "I don't trust you."

"I like that, too. And I'm willing to work for your trust. Don't make any decisions now. Let's clear Hugh's name, you'll see what kind of an organization we are, what we can do, and you might like it."

I wanted to accuse him of setting the whole thing up, of dragging me here and using Hugh as a magnet but I held my tongue and turned to my salad instead. "Do you know much about Miami history?" Bobby asked, breaking the silence between us.

"No."

"It wasn't founded until 1896..." As he started to share the history of his city, developed by an enterprising railroad tycoon, I thought of Kurt Jessup's lecture to me on New York right before the bastard attempted to strangle me to death.

"You have a lot in common with Kurt, don't you?" I asked, interrupting him.

He paused, fork raised in the air, a beet skewered in its tongs. "We were friends, and for a long time I thought we wanted the same thing, but I was wrong."

I sneered. "Wrong?"

Bobby put down his fork. "He liked pain, that's not my game. I like control, often both desires express themselves similarly. You're more like me, control is what you're after."

"I just want to live a quiet life."

"No, you don't," he smiled at me. "Not in the least. You want to control things, you want to make them right, as you see it. So do I."

"You're fighting for what's right?"

"As I see it."

"You seem more motivated by money and power than good."

"Who says they have to be mutually exclusive?"

"Laws of nature."

"Ah, now you want to talk about the laws of nature? Let me ask you this then. Who made the wretched so wretched? God?"

"I don't believe in God, and if I did, I'd think he was a real prick. If God's the one fucking with us I'd like to kick him in his nuts."

He laughed. "I bet you'd get him. But, if not God, who or what is doing it then?"

"Men like you," I said before I could stop myself.

"You think I'm that powerful?"

"I know you are. You can make people disappear. Look what you've done for me."

"Yes," he smiled. "Look at what I did for you. I'm glad we can both recognize the favors I've bestowed on you."

The door opened with a swish against the carpeted floor and the maid reentered, clearing our plates. "Wine, please," Bobby said to her without taking his eyes off me. The flames from the candles flickered, casting shadows across his face, dancing like jesters for his amusement. The woman nodded and left us again.

Bobby leaned forward. "We were talking about the favors I've done for you."

"Favors?" I sat forward matching his posture.

"I suppose I should feel lucky you have not retaliated," he said.

I didn't answer but nodded slightly.

His lips slid back into that smile, the one where he looked like a snake and a panther all wrapped up into one venomous dangerous creature. "You're probably right," he said. "I should be careful with you." He licked his lips. "Sydney, I'd like to watch you go for anything, even if it's my life. Passion suits you."

My dress suddenly felt too tight, the candles too close, my chair too small. I took several deep breaths, steadying myself. The door opened again and I sat back, smiling at the maid as she placed a plate with lamb chops, scalloped potatoes, and cooked spinach in front of me. "I hope you like lamb," Bobby said. "Some people have an ethical objection to it."

Before I could answer, Claude came in. Robert looked up at him and they shared a silent communication. "I'm sorry," he said. "I've got to take a phone call."

"You know what?" I said, standing. "That's fine. I'm gonna go." Blue came out from under the table, his ears perked, watching me closely.

Robert stood as well, buttoning his suit jacket. "If you must."

"Yeah, I think it's best," I said with a smile.

"Please, keep the car."

I opened my mouth to protest but he cut me off.

"At least until you leave Miami," he smiled. "Please." He reached down and picked up the copy of *The Prince*. "Don't forget this."

I took it from him. "Fine," I said, taking a step back, Blue staying close. "I can show myself out."

He nodded. "As you wish."

EK

I pulled open the large wooden door, feeling strange without an escort. Like I was sneaking out, leaving without my host's permission. But there was part of me that knew that was impossible. Bobby could do what he wanted. I was free because that's how he wanted me. For now.

Blue jumped over my seat and into the passenger side. I pushed the button in the center console, the Audi's lights lit the drive and its engine turned on with a rumble that suggested power and strength. It filled me with a sense of success, a feeling that somehow I'd made it, and I understood why people bought expensive cars. They weren't just for show. They were for real.

I hit the gas and my tires squealed as I pulled out of the driveway. The gate was open and I turned back onto the main road, past the park, and right up to the gatehouse. For a moment I wondered if the arm would rise. I slowed down and rolled toward the barrier at an idle. It began to move with a jerk and I pushed the gas, not waiting for the arm to reach its apex before leaving the island behind.

I decided to head back to the hotel because I didn't know what else to do. The trip was short and I left the Audi where I'd gotten it, sitting in the hotel's drive. The valet smiled at me knowingly. It had all been arranged. I was special.

Blue and I went up to the room. I took off the dress and walked into the bathroom wearing just my bra, panties, and knife. I took a moment to look in the mirror, to make eye contact, to try to ground myself within myself. 'I was not like Bobby Maxim' I wanted to hear back from my reflection. I was different. Better. But the look that came back didn't make anything clearer. My gray eyes looked dangerous, impervious.

A knock at the door broke my gaze. I grabbed a robe, wrapping myself up in it, as I went to answer.

CHAPTER SEVEN
DARKNESS CALLS

Dan started talking as soon as I opened the door.

"I'm sorry about earlier. I didn't come here to fight with you." He looked down at Blue who pushed his muzzle against Dan's thigh. Looking back at me, his head still bent down, he continued, "I need to tell you something. It's important and I, I guess it's still just a little rawer than I thought." He rubbed the back of his neck and smiled at me, looking like a boy who'd done wrong.

"Fine," I said, stepping aside. "Come in." I pushed the door open wider and he entered.

"Want a drink?" I asked.

"Sure, thanks."

I went over to the bar and grabbed a mini bottle of Maker's Mark, tossing it to him. He caught it and unscrewed the cap, the cracking of the plastic matching the tension in the room.

"So what did you need to tell me?" I asked as I watched him take a sip, his lips wrapping around the small opening.

He brought the bottle down and took a breath before answering. "Joyful Justice is happening."

"What does that mean?" I asked, feeling a chill in my gut.

"Me, some others. We're doing it with or without you."

"When was this decided?" I asked, the coldness spreading to my limbs.

"Does it matter when?"

I didn't answer, my mind reeling. It felt like I'd been sucked out of a plane, the world depressurized, whirling out of control, falling quickly down.

"The point is we want to help with Hugh," Dan continued. He reached into his back pocket and pulled out folded sheets of paper. Holding them up he said, "I got some info on Robert Maxim if you want to see."

He unfolded the paper and sat on the couch. Dan patted the seat next to him and smiled. "Don't worry, I don't bite." I didn't move. "On paper he looks like a pretty good guy," Dan said, looking down at his notes.

"Wait," I said, holding out a palm. Dan paused. "When did this happen?"

Dan licked his lips. "When we were in India."

"When?" I asked, my voice hoarse.

"When we were together, the whole time, we've been working on it."

"The whole time?" I asked. "You were keeping this from me the whole time?"

He nodded. My mind raced over those months, flashing onto our bodies in the sun, a hash joint hanging from my lips, the musky flavor filling my mouth, Dan's kiss, our touch. None of it held any promises but to enjoy each other. Honesty, truth, they'd never been in the bargain. "Right," I said. "We never made any promises."

Dan nodded again, slowly. "And that's why I have no reason to be angry with you and you have no reason to be angry with me. We can be friends."

"Friends?" I asked.

"Partners, even," he said. "Have you thought about it?"

I opened my mouth and closed it again, shaking my head. "I have not had enough time. It's all been so..." I played with the knot of my bathrobe. "Quick." I felt the clench of tears in my throat and looked down at my feet. Shit, I could not start crying right now.

"I wasn't supposed to tell you about this," Dan said.

I didn't answer as water welled in my eyes, making my feet and the golden carpeting blur beneath me. I heard Dan stand up and cross the room. He put an arm around my shoulders and I shuddered in a breath, trying to gain control over my feelings. Part of it, I realized, was relief. I had not betrayed Dan.

"Hey," Dan said, squeezing my shoulders. "It's okay, you don't have to decide this now." He kissed the top of my head. I blinked and the tears dropped from my eyes, landing on the tie of my robe. "Let's just help Hugh and then we can talk about it, okay?"

I nodded and swiped at my eyes, desperate to end this conversation, to talk about something else. Stepping away from Dan's arm, I went over to the couch. "Show me what you've got on Maxim," I said, sitting down.

"There is not a whole lot." Dan handed over his typed notes and sat down next to me. "But I'm digging deeper, getting into his personal stuff, deeper into what Fortress Global is doing, but it's going to be hard. Not impossible but it will take time and money."

"You have access to my bank accounts, use whatever you need," I said, looking down at the pages of charities Maxim supported on his last tax return.

"Yes," Dan said. "I will take what I need." I looked up at him and he smiled. I turned away from his beautiful green eyes, returning my attention to the papers. I placed my free hand in the space between us trying to create a barrier.

"Robert Maxim has complete control over FGI, no board, no nothing. He built it from scratch and he's never needed any investors."

"Is he from money?" I asked.

Dan shook his head. "His mom was a piano teacher and his dad owned a tailor shop in South Beach."

"So where did the money come from?" I asked.

Dan shrugged. "I'd guess drugs. This city, a whole hell of a lot of it was built with trafficking money. It was by far the largest sector of the economy for a long time. Some of FGI's first big clients had known links to organized crime, cartels."

I nodded. "Right, makes sense."

"I've only skimmed the surface, but from what I can see nothing points to why Robert would set up Hugh."

"Me, it's me he's after. I'm the reason he would set up Hugh," I answered, not taking my eyes off the list of charities.

"I believe that," Dan said. I looked up at him and immediately down again. Scooting away from him, I stood. "I've got to get some sleep," I said, not feeling tired but knowing that I couldn't continue with Dan in my room. "You should go," I said, making eye contact.

He nodded and stood. "Okay." Dan reached into his front pocket and pulled out what looked like a square piece of plastic. "This is for you," he said, handing it to me. It was smooth and lightweight. "It blocks listening devices and trackers," Dan said, then smiled. "Well, not my trackers, but most people's."

"You think this place is bugged?" I asked.

Dan laughed. "Uh, yeah. Just keep it on you and you'll be safe wherever you go."

"Thanks," I said, looking up at him.

Dan reached out and gently took hold of the end of my bathrobe belt. "See you soon," he said, rubbing it between his fingers for a moment before turning and leaving. I stared at the closed door and felt an intense need to get the fuck out of there.

EK

I pulled on a pair of wrinkled jeans that smelled like the smoke of burning plastic, incense, and hash. They hadn't been worn since India. I threw on a white T-shirt. Grabbing my bag, I dropped the device Dan gave me into it. Robert Maxim's key fob was already inside. Downstairs my car was where I'd left it and, with a nod to the valet, I motioned for Blue to jump in. He passed over my seat into the passenger's. I opened the sunroof and he raised his nose, sniffing at the night air.

The car rumbled at the curb as I sat there wondering where to go. Deciding I wanted to get out of the city I searched through my bag until I found the details about where Lawrence Taggert's body was found. I put the coordinates into the GPS and then followed directions as it led me through South Beach. The streets were packed with people, their bodies tight and exposed. Girls balancing on high heels, their boyfriends, in button-down shirts and ironed jeans holding onto them as they pushed through the tables that lined the sidewalks making navigation that much more difficult. Some of the people pressed into the streets dangerously unsteady.

Blue watched it all, occasionally raising his face to the skylight for a sniff of what I'll never know. I squeezed the wheel of the car, wanting to be going fast, turn quickly, anything to make my mind concentrate on things besides the raging emotions inside of me. Eventually we made it to SW 8th Street where we turned west. On the causeway we cruised over the bay, past downtown where FGI's building stood in a cluster with other skyscrapers. They looked imposing against the flat landscape of southern Florida. I weaved between cars, picking up speed. We drove onto one of those roads that is found in every part of the United States. Lined with fast food restaurants, gas stations, and big box stores. Clogged with lights that always seem to turn red as we approached.

I banged my hand against the wheel. To our left was a casino where rich rewards were promised on large signs that flashed into the night. Before us was the Everglades and, as the light turned green I took off, speeding into the welcome darkness of the wild.

Within a couple of miles the landscape and the sky became one black mass beyond the reach of my headlights. Low and bright they lit the reflectors on the road and the guardrail, occasionally catching the swaying grasses beyond. In my rearview mirror the city's lights made the low clouds glow burgundy. A truck rumbled past me, headed to the city. Its windshield was dark, the high headlights illuminating the canal that slunk slowly by to my right.

Up ahead, bright white lights pooled around a tall power grid structure. At its entrance, a bridge crossed the canal allowing access to the facility. A dirt road continued on that side, running parallel with the paved one we raced upon. On our left, yellow street lights clustered around a closed Gator Park that advertised airboat rides. Then darkness again. Another Gator Park, this one advertising an Indian Village. The next cluster of lights was the gas station and convenience store Hugh stopped at. I pulled in and parked. Blue followed me out, and I let him pee on the grass before putting him back in the car.

Inside the gas station was a familiar array of amenities. The shelves and coolers were well stocked with chips, candy bars, and sodas. Hot dogs spun in their own grease beneath the warming heat of long, yellow bulbs. I tonged one of the frankfurters and placed it into a bun, soft to the touch yet dry on the exterior, left out in the air for too long.

I grabbed two bottles of water from the cooler. A bag of Twizzlers caught my attention as I walked back toward the checkout. A Sikh stood behind the counter, his turban bright orange, fitting in nicely with the multi-colored cigarette packs and lottery cards that he stood in front of.

"Hi," I said with a smile.

"Good evening," he nodded as I pushed my purchase across the counter. I guessed he was in his mid-forties, circles under his eyes made it clear that it was close to midnight and he worked under fluorescent lights. He smiled. "You don't like ketchup?"

I shrugged. "It's actually for my dog."

He laughed and shook his head. "My name's Sydney," I offered, and held out my hand.

He cocked his head but reached across to shake. "Sanjit," he said.

"I'm a private investigator, and I'm working on the Lawrence Taggert case."

He nodded and frowned, leaning ever so slightly away from me. "I was not here and I've already handed over the surveillance video."

"Thanks, I've seen some of it. I was wondering if you knew how much gas he bought?"

The man's eyes opened wider. "Why do you want to know that?" he asked.

I sighed. "It seems, from watching the video—did you watch it?" I asked. He nodded. "Right, so to me, it didn't seem like he put much gas in the car and he didn't come inside."

"No, he never came inside."

"Right, so why did he stop? If he didn't *need* the gas."

He pursed his lips. "He did not buy very much. Only $10." He shook his head side to side. "I also thought it strange. Why would a man do this? With another man in his trunk?" Sanjit's frown deepened, large creases appearing between his eyebrows.

"That's what I'm saying."

"But," Sanjit held up his hands. "I don't want to get involved."

"Of course not," I said, shaking my head. "You're not involved at all." He nodded, somewhat reassured and began to put my water and Twizzlers into a bag. "Do you have access to more surveillance footage?" I asked.

"I already gave the whole week to the police," he said, turning to the register.

"I was hoping to look further back."

"I'm not sure if that's allowed."

"Perfectly legal."

"I keep 90 days." His eyes narrowed, thinking.

"I can pay you," I offered. His eyes attached to mine, insult clear across his face. "Or you can do it for the good of justice," I offered with a smile.

"Come back in an hour. I will have my son put it onto a thumb drive for you." He turned around and unhooked a package behind him, running it under the scanner. I handed over my credit card. "My son was here," Sanjit said, "when he came."

"I know," I said, having read it in Antonio's report.

"You think he didn't do it?" Sanjit asked.

"I'm determined to find out who did."

EK

Back in the car I headed for the spot where Taggert's corpse was found. My GPS took me straight to the public launch site where, according to evidence, Hugh had pulled over, let Lawrence out of the trunk, knocked him to his knees, shot him once in the side of the head, and then kicked his body down the cement ramp into the shallow waters.

I sat in the car, the headlights cutting through the thick darkness over the cement ramp and into the trees beyond. They were Everglade apple trees according to the file. Taggert's body became tangled in them. The trees grew tightly together, their roots intertwining, growing over and around each other so that you could hardly tell which limb belonged to which tree. Each year when they shed their leaves they fell upon the bed of roots and over decades they formed a hammock. A place where deer and other wildlife lived, above the water of the Everglades. The trees fluttered in the wind, their leaves twinkling silver-green in the blue glare of my headlights. I stared into the darkness between the trunks; it looked impenetrable.

I climbed out and Blue followed. The water was still and black, somehow even darker than the night around us. On its surface, lilies floated, their night blooms yellow and vivid against the inky water. The car engine and bright lights seemed to make the place into a theater, the engine's rumble the murmur of the audience, waiting for something to happen. The frogs and insects' calls the sound of the orchestra tuning up.

I walked over to the cement ramp. There was no sign of blood, but then again, something as nutritious as that would not sit around for long in a swamp. A sound, a splash in the water, released a low growl from Blue and raised goosebumps across my skin. "It's probably just a frog," I said, but I felt eyes on me and backed toward the car. Blue hopped in first and I followed, closing the door blocking out the night sounds and cocooning me in rich leather and luxury.

Turning back onto the long, straight, and unbelievably flat road, I headed toward the city, my destination made obvious by the light pollution that haunted the horizon.

Pulling back into the gas station I found Sanjit's son listening to his iPod and eating a hot dog. When he saw me the young man pulled off his headphones. "Hi," he said with his mouth still half-full.

"Hi, I was here earlier talking with your dad. He said that I could stop back in and pick up your security footage."

The young man, brown skin, tall and lanky, not yet grown into his broad shoulders or big feet, nodded and swallowed. Putting down the hot dog he stood and picked up the thumb drive his father had sold me earlier that night. "I put it all on here."

"You were here that night, right?" I asked.

He nodded, his face falling. "Yeah, I feel real bad that I didn't notice. But you know, the guy didn't come in or anything. He paid with his card at the pump. How would I have known?"

"It's not your fault," I said. "Trust me. There is nothing you could have done."

"But if I'd noticed, I could have called the police," he said, his eyes widening with the truth of it. His pain was obvious and I didn't know how to help him. There are all sorts of casualties, all sorts of pain that come from violent death that cannot be measured or foreseen.

"You're helping now," I said, taking the thumb drive from him.

"I hope you get the guy," the kid said, his brow furrowing with anger.

"Thanks again," I said as I left, the bell on the door tolling my exit.

CHAPTER EIGHT
NIGHT OUT

Back in South Beach I parked the car in my spot and was crossing through the lobby when I heard and felt the humming of the bar. I followed the sounds and found myself in a room with tall ceilings, Liberace-style chandeliers, and young people gyrating. I pushed through the crowd to the bar and ordered a tequila from the woman who tended it. As I sipped the liquor, which burned me just right, I looked out into the crowd.

Maybe they all looked so good through gentle, persistent encouragement from friends and family but I didn't really believe that's how humans worked. Those carved bodies spoke of hours of hard labor, sweat, heavy breathing, and pure will. If you couldn't handle it, you left. Or became rich and then it didn't matter how flabby your ass or abs. Money made you beautiful.

"Another," I mouthed to the bartender and gently tapped the bar with my pointer finger. She handed over two beers to a customer and then returned to me, tequila bottle in hand. A guy leaned too close to me and Blue growled, causing the man to jump back, hands up to his chest, baseball cap coming askew. "Whoa," he laughed. "That dog is cute."

"He bites," I said, looking up at him.

"Sorry," he mumbled before stepping back into the crowded push of bodies.

The bartender leaned against the bar, careful not to touch its sticky surface. "You're not very good at making friends," she said, her lips close to my ear.

I couldn't help but smile. "You're right," I answered. She held my gaze, her eyes were green and lined with black charcoal that bled into the thin lines beneath her bottom lashes, mingling with sweat from the hard work she did. "Do you want to be my friend?" I asked, feeling bold.

She smiled and shrugged a bare shoulder. "I get off at 4. Let's see if you're still around." Then she returned her attention to the clamoring patrons who pushed against the bar, arms out, dollars fisted, brows red with excitement, alcohol, and dance. I shot the tequila and left the glass sitting on a $100 bill, then slipped back into the crowd, Blue following me like a tail.

On the street, crowds of people smoked and laughed. I turned off the main drag and into a quieter lane. I stepped around a large puddle that looked like a muddy mirror until Blue stepped right in it. "Oh, come on," I said, looking down at his brown paws. "Every puddle, Blue, every puddle?" He looked up at me, not seeing the problem. I began to walk again but Blue's growl stopped me. I turned to see three figures coming around the corner. In the lead was a short, curvy girl, a peroxide blonde wearing a bronze spray tan and a hot pink mini dress. It squeezed her under the arms causing small rolls of fat to pop out. Her breasts did a bit of popping, too.

She stopped several yards away from me, her girlfriends fanning out in some kind of tableau of a western movie street scene. They, too, wore club clothes and bare feet. I wondered, for a moment, what they did with their heels until I noticed pinky was holding a knife. Tiny and silly, she held it out in the light, showing it off, as though Blue and I might find her intimidating.

"Are you actually planning on fighting me and my dog?" I asked them, noticing a small slur in my speech.

"If that dog bites us, he'll be put down," she said and then brought her lips together into a little kiss. They were smudged with red lipstick like she'd been making out right before coming out here to kick my ass.

"Did you just threaten my dog?" I asked, adrenaline chasing the slur from my words. Something in my tone and the coldness in my eyes made her falter. "How about you just apologize," I said, "and we can all continue with our night."

"No, no," she said, taking two indignant, heavy steps that sounded big but didn't close the space between us. "You'll apologize to me for what your dog did to my man!"

I could not help but laugh. She stared at me and her two friends exchanged glances. "Sorry," I managed to say. "That is just too funny. I feel like I'm on a reality show. Do you ever watch those? They are always having crazy fights on the street and pulling each other's hair out." My phone rang, but I didn't take my eyes off the girl in front of me. "Are you going to try to rip out my hair now?" She rocked back and forth, switching her weight from one foot to the other. "You'll have to get closer," I told her. She chewed on her bottom lip, scraping off the last of the red lipstick clinging there.

"Fuck it," I said, and in two easy steps closed the distance between us. Extending my left arm, turning my body sideways to narrow her target area, I grabbed a clump of the girl's hair right at the apex of her forehead. Twisting my body hard, I ripped out the hair and brought my right fist around in a cross strike that knocked the girl off her feet. Before she touched the pavement I'd already backed up next to Blue, holding the bloody clump of blonde hair. When she did hit the ground, she stayed there.

Having their leader knocked out cold left the other two girls with a dilemma. "You can take her and go," I said. They cautiously moved toward the small pink figure. Each grabbed her under an arm and began to lift. She moaned and her head lolled on her neck, blood dripped down her face. As I watched them leave the alley, Blue turned and I heard clapping. I swiveled and dropped low at the same time. Blue took off toward the figure who, when she stepped into the light, I recognized as my old friend, Malina.

"Same old Sydney Rye," she said in her light Mexican accent.

I stood up and walked to meet her, dropping the clump of hair on the ground. Blue pranced around Malina and she stopped clapping to give him the greeting he expected. Kisses on the face and ruffling of the ears. "Malina," I said, pulling her into a hug. "It's great to see you." Blue pushed between us with a low yowl of protest and we both laughed, breaking apart.

Malina looked dazzling as she almost always did. Long dark hair falling in large waves over her shoulders, glittering almond shaped eyes, flawless skin. She wore a belted rain coat, her legs bare, and low heels that, on her, looked sexy.

"How did you find me?" I asked.

"Dan," she said. "You know he tracks you."

I laughed. "Is that creepy?"

She shrugged. "You ask me, it's romantic but..." Malina laughed.

I put an arm around her. "Let's get a drink."

"Yes, someplace quiet. We need to talk."

EK

"You remember the first time we met?" Malina asked, looking around the bar.

"Pretty different than this," I answered, remembering the tourist trap in Puerto Penasco where our beers wept onto the table and Malina was allowed to smoke. Her best friend recently murdered, Malina fought back tears and danced with men for money while I stewed over the injustices of the world and my inability to do anything about them.

Our waitress this evening was almost as scantily clad as the one who'd served us that night. We ordered two cognacs, it seemed appropriate with the late hour and sultry decor of the bar. "How are those girls?" I asked after the waitress, wearing fishnet stockings and black silk short shorts, left us with our drinks. I took a sip, the strong liquor filled my nose and pricked at my eyes.

"Good," she said. "Lenox took them to a non-profit that specializes in helping victims of sex trade traffic get green cards and rebuild their lives.

And he cleaned up your mess. Both guys survived and neither of them is admitting a woman got the best of them."

"What were they doing with those girls?"

"Making them work in clubs, dance, suck dick, what do you think, Sydney?"

"Guessing those guys weren't the masterminds behind the operation."

"I could ask Lenox for a name."

"Lenox?" I asked. "The man on the phone?"

"Devastatingly handsome and sexy man." Malina fanned herself. "You're lucky you didn't meet him, what with your already tangled romantic life." I flinched and Malina cleared her throat. "I've known him for about two years."

"He's in your business?"

She smiled. "Yes, but he specializes in the opposite sex.'

"Men."

She nodded. "And he believes strongly in human rights on both sides of the marketplace."

"Very noble."

"He is quite a man."

I laughed. "I'm sure."

There was a pause during which Malina chewed on her bottom lip. "What?" I asked.

"Dan wasn't supposed to tell you."

"You too, Malina?"

"You don't want to join us, Dan says."

"I don't know what it is," I answered honestly, sitting back into the deep booth, feeling safe and hidden behind its high back and curved wall.

"You can't expect us all to go back to our lives, Sydney. We are hungry. You know?"

Someone laughed a little too loud, as though they were listening, and agreed how ridiculous that sounded.

"Malina, come on," I said, sitting forward. "You're a pragmatist. I can't believe you really agree with Dan. You know it's called Joyful Justice?"

"Yes," she leaned back. "I know. I like it." Her nose wrinkled as though she was looking at something cute.

"What is your plan, though? What are you going to do, take on all the evil in the world?"

Malina shrugged. "We'll take on what we can."

"So what you're talking about is coordinating a vigilante network?"

"I knew you'd get it."

I laughed. "Malina, I do not get it."

She sat forward quickly, reaching out and grabbing onto my hand. "Yes, you do, Sydney. You know what I'm talking about. There is grave injustice in this world and together, we can change that."

"You and me?"

"There are many of us."

I thought about Santiago, the sultry voice of Lenox on the phone, and all the other people on the Joyful Justice website. Could all of them agree with Malina? "You are no different," Malina said. "Look at what you did this afternoon."

"That's different, Malina, it happened right in front of me."

"So it's fine as long as you don't see it?"

"No," I answered. "It's not."

"Then what is stopping you? Why won't you join us?"

I sat back again, taking my drink with me and stared down into the translucent caramel liquid. "How do you know it will be better?"

"Of course it will be better," Malina said with absolute conviction. "How could it be worse?"

"But how will you do it, Malina? How will you accomplish such a lofty goal?" I looked up from the cognac feeling deeply tired, the jet lag hitting me like a freight train. "How many people will have to die?"

Malina leaned forward, the candlelight playing across her exquisite features. "It's a means to a just end, Sydney."

I winced.

"What?"

"You just sound a little bit too much like someone else right now." I stood up. "I'm exhausted. I can't talk about this anymore."

Malina stood as well. "You're right. It's late. We can talk more later." I started to turn toward the exit but she stopped me, reaching out and holding my wrist. Her fingers were smooth and cool. "We're not leaving."

"What do you mean?"

"Dan, me, your friends. Members of Joyful Justice. We are not giving up on you. We will stay here and help."

"I don't know what you can do."

She smiled and put an arm around my shoulder, directing us through the door. "We will see."

EK

I took off my jeans and T-shirt leaving them bunched on the floor. I showered, washing away the small spatter of blood on my wrist from yanking out that girl's hair. Jesus, that was stupid, I thought. Was Robert right about me? Was I some power hungry psycho?

I tried not to think about it, turning my mind instead to Malina's appearance, her insistence that the world could be a better place if only someone did something. If *we* did something. Those thoughts also hurt my brain so I pushed them aside. I dried off quickly and ran the blow dryer over my hair enough so that I hoped not to wake up in the morning looking like a complete freak.

Climbing into bed I turned off the lights. Blue jumped up and after circling three times settled at my feet, his chin resting across one of my ankles. I looked down at him and admired his ability to just fall asleep. Blue wasn't worried about justice, evil, anything. But then again maybe he had me to do all that for him. Maybe I needed a me and that brought my brain back around to Bobby Maxim and I sat up and turned on the light. Finding the TV controller I clicked it on and then climbed out of bed and found the copy of THE PRINCE that Maxim had given to me.

Back in bed I cracked the cover. *For my Princess.* Ugh, did he actually write that? Gross. I started reading but as my eyes tried to focus on the words I slipped into a deep sleep with the light and TV on.

CHAPTER NINE
TIME FOR SOME DETECTING

I woke to a strange sound. Something like humming, singing, and vibrating all combined. Blinking my eyes, I saw light streaming through the slit between the curtains. The vibrating stopped but the humming/singing continued. I looked up at the TV where a group of men sat around a camp fire. "Throat Singing," the announcer said, "was popular in Genghis' camp and is still heard across the Mongolian steppes to this day."

Blue, still curled at the end of the bed, watched me. The vibrating started again and I fished around in the bedding until I found my phone, Mulberry's name on the screen. "Hey," I said, my voice still rough from sleep.

"Hey," he said, his voice soft. I found the controller and muted the TV.

"Did I wake you?"

"Yes, but it's fine."

"How did it go last night?"

I sat up and watched the mute television. Large men on small horses galloped across an open field, bearing down on several yurts where women and children in traditional Mongolian dress waited, huddled together and frightened.

"I'll meet you where we jogged the other day." I looked over at the clock. It was three in the afternoon. Jet lag, old buddy, old pal. "Give me forty-five minutes," I said.

"Fine, don't forget we have another strategy meeting this evening."

"Okay," I said, throwing my legs over the side of the bed. Blue jumped down and stretched, waving his tail in the air and letting out a yowl with his yawn.

"See you soon."

We hung up and I quickly brushed my teeth and put on my jogging clothing.

Mulberry was waiting for us when Blue and I jogged up. I plucked my headphones from my ears and smiled at him feeling good after my run.

"Sydney," Mulberry looked like he wanted to reach out and hug me. He was in jeans and a loose black T-shirt made of a material that both managed to hang loosely and yet show off the definition of his shoulders and chest. "How did it go last night?"

I stayed out of Mulberry's reach and dragged my eyes off his body and up to his eyes, but they were shining in a way that made me turn to the sea.

"He said something that made me think my room is bugged," I answered and then turned back to him. "Something about how it's not fair that women get called sluts when men can do what they like."

It was Mulberry's turn to look away. "Sorry about yesterday."

"Yeah?" I said, crossing my arms.

Mulberry ran a hand through his hair, the smattering of silver caught the bright sunlight even in the shade of the tree we stood beneath. "I don't think you're a slut," he said, not looking at me.

I nodded. "I don't think you're in love with me," I said. "I'm sorry I said that." He looked back at me. I licked my lips, my mouth suddenly feeling dry, leaving me thirsty. "I'm sorry," I said again, biting down on my bottom lip administering a flick of pain. Mulberry turned away first, walking to the stone wall and staring out at the ocean.

I stepped toward him. "Look," I said. "We need to work together to clear Hugh's name, but I need you to know that Robert Maxim is not to be trusted."

Mulberry sighed. "Because he said you weren't a slut."

"No, because he is after me."

Mulberry turned to me, his eyes dark with anger. "I know that, Sydney. You don't think I know how much he wants you. He wants you to work with him—,"

"And that's why he set up Hugh," I interrupted him, "and is listening to our conversations."

Mulberry sighed in frustration, turned away and then back to me, opened his mouth, but didn't speak.

"What?" I said.

He pursed his lips. "Nothing," he said, shaking his head.

"What were you and Dan talking about?" I asked him. He looked up at me, his eyes unreadable. "I saw you talking after I left."

"I apologized," Mulberry answered, taking his time with each syllable, watching for my reaction.

"Why would you need to apologize to him?"

Mulberry ran his hand through his hair again and didn't make eye contact. "I knew how he felt about you."

"You two talked, when we were in India?"

"Malina and I were in touch," Mulberry answered, avoiding my gaze.

"Malina?" I asked.

"After Mexico, we stayed in touch, she's an incredible lady," Mulberry said. "Why wouldn't I stay in touch with her?" He lifted himself taller as though I was accusing him of something.

"No reason," I said, shaking my head. I wanted to ask him what he knew about Joyful Justice, but I couldn't. I didn't want to know. Which side he came down on meant too much to me. I couldn't let it sway me.

"We never talked about it," Mulberry said.

"It?" I asked, looking up at him, wondering if he had read my mind. He caught my elbow.

"Did it mean anything to you?" he asked, his face tight.

I realized he was talking about the other "it". I couldn't look at him and pulled free. "Of course," I answered, my mind transporting me back to my hotel suite in Udaipur, Mulberry's rough hands against my skin, fighting me as hard as I fought him. It was so raw. Then lying in his arms, feeling incredibly safe. I felt my face flush.

"But you don't trust me?" he asked, his voice low, almost a whisper, like he didn't want the truth to permeate the air with all its horrible facts.

"You think I don't want to?" I asked him, anger edging my voice. "You think I like keeping my distance from you? I don't. I need you now more than ever." My voice broke and he reached out for me but I backed away shaking my head. Clearing my throat I continued, "I don't want to make a mistake that will cost me my life and Hugh his freedom."

"Sydney, how could you think I would do anything to hurt you?"

I wet my lips. "I don't know what's between you and Robert. But I know he's no good for me. That if he had his way, I'd become something I don't want to be."

Mulberry ran a hand through his hair, leaving the curls standing on end. "I'm sorry, Sydney. I wish you could trust me."

"Me, too. We should go," I said, turning back toward the hotel. "We have a meeting to attend. And I've got to get some clothing."

"Didn't you go shopping?" Mulberry called after me as I jogged away.

When I walked into the strategy meeting, Ashley and Antonio were already there. They both smiled and we greeted each other. The building across the way glowed pink and violet in the twilight.

I was wearing a pair of tight white jeans, desert boots, and a gray T-shirt that I'd bought on my way back from the jog. They fit pretty well considering I hadn't tried any of them on. But I still looked casual next to Antonio and Ashley with their pressed jackets and collared shirts.

Before the inane chitchat could begin, Mulberry walked in. He looked over at us, a scowl on his brow. Ashley's eyes were watching him, smiling and flirty. She batted her lashes as she said, "Hi," in a husky tone.

"Ashley," he nodded. "Let's get right to it. You have a report."

"Yes," she answered, stepping to the front of the room. Ashley waited for the rest of us to take our seats. No Edwards or Maxim today, I noted.

"I've been digging into Mr. Taggert's finances," Ashley began, "and have discovered the man had a serious gambling problem. And he wasn't playing craps at the Indian Casino."

I remembered seeing a casino on the road to the Everglades, right at the edge of civilization. It offered the dream of a big win, a ticket to the good life.

"He was playing in Ivan Zhovra's poker games." The screen behind her lit up with a picture of a big man, Slavic and scary looking, crossing a street with a shorter, just as dangerous looking, man. "Zhovra's taken a bigger chunk of illegal gambling in this city over the past three years than any other organization. He is ruthless and suspected in several murders." The screen lit up with the photo of a dead man, his eyes open and glazed white, half buried in wet sand.

"Zhovra also owns a string of strip clubs across the state. He is suspected of trafficking girls from Russia and other ex-Soviet nations." I sat forward. "Last year, Zhovra started showing up at *Defry's*. I found him on tapes going back to the first week." The screen showed Ivan Zhovra sitting at a table with Hugh, who wore his chef's smock, and Taggert in a shiny gray suit. The white tablecloth that lay before them was stained with circles of red wine and splotches of dark sauces, all evidence of a meal well enjoyed. As were the smiles on all three men's faces.

"Then, in the past four months, Ivan has been eating at *Defry's* more regularly, and from the cursory examination we've been able to do on the bills, not paying for anything. All of his meals have been put onto Taggert's personal account. I have an appointment with Mr. Defry tomorrow to find out what he knows about the two men's relationships, but, I think at this point we can certainly consider Ivan Zhovra as a suspect."

"Ivan Zhovra," I whispered to myself.

"Did you say something?" Mulberry asked.

I looked over at him. "Do you think Lawrence was involved with the girls?"

Ashley answered me. "We don't have anything to confirm or deny that at the moment, but I think he was mainly a gambler."

"There is no way Hugh would have gone along with it," I said. "He wouldn't have let them use his restaurant as a cover."

Antonio cleared his throat and adjusted in his chair. I looked over at him, raising my eyebrows. "Seems to me," he said, "we shouldn't avoid any avenue of investigation. You never know what you might find while looking for something else."

"You're right," I said. "We must be fearless with our inquiry, no matter where it leads."

Antonio's brows twitched into a frown, but then reset themselves as he gave a friendly smile and nodded.

"Any other questions?" Mulberry asked, looking around the table, his eyebrows raised. When no one spoke, he said, "All right, Sydney and I will go and interview Ivan tomorrow. We can also see Hugh beforehand. So Ashley, you just keep going through those tapes."

Ashley tried to cover up her disappointment, but there was no denying the falter in her smile, the tightness around her eyes. I felt a pang in my stomach recognizing that she'd done the work, found the lead, and now she had to sit on the sidelines. I hated that shit.

Pulling the thumb drive out of my bag, I offered it to Mulberry, as Ashley took her seat. "I went by the gas station last night, where Hugh stopped on his way to the Everglades, and got their footage for the past six months."

Mulberry cocked his head at me, questioning when I'd gone out to the gas station, but didn't say anything. His fingers brushed against mine as he took the small object from me. He passed it on to Ashley. "Take this to the viewing room with you. I'll stop by tomorrow."

"Also," I said. "Hugh only put about $10 in his tank."

"That's right," Ashley said. "$10.80. I checked his credit card statement."

"So, that's definitely weird. Even the guy at the gas station agreed."

"I'll pass it on to Edwards," Ashley said.

"Fine," Mulberry said. "What about the tox screen?"

"Came back totally negative," Ashley said.

"Have you spoken to Edwards about it?" Mulberry asked.

"He says it must be something they don't normally test for."

"Right," Mulberry said and then turned to Antonio. "What have you got?"

"I spoke to Taggert's wife. She was in Africa on a safari and only got home three days ago. She is making the funeral arrangements but seems in okay spirits. Wearing all black and looking good in it." Antonio glanced down at his iPad. "She couldn't think of why anyone would want to kill her husband and was shocked that Hugh would do a thing like this. She'd only met him a couple of times but he seemed, 'very sweet'."

"Do you think she knew about the gambling?" I asked.

Antonio looked up at me. "I'm guessing no, but I'll ask her. She is loaded. Her family owns Tenson Pharmaceuticals. She travels a lot, a lady of leisure if you will," Antonio said with a smile. "They didn't spend much time together."

"So she doesn't work in the family business?"

"She's one of the members of the board and does a lot of work with the family foundation."

"The foundation?"

Antonio nodded and began flipping through his iPad again. "Yeah, they provide free vaccines around the world and also put some money into research. Apparently Lawrence was also passionate about the foundation and organized the gala every year."

"Do you think she was involved?" Mulberry asked. "Gut feeling."

Antonio shrugged. "She seemed to have genuine affection for him, if not true love. She said he was fun and easy to be married to. Didn't tell her what to do."

"Hmm," I said. "I can get that."

"Me too," Ashley said, and then immediately turned bright red, her eyes darting around the table, surprised she'd spoken aloud.

CHAPTER TEN
THE DEVIL'S BREATH

I called Lenox. "Sydney," he said. "I hoped you would call." His voice was as good as I remembered it.

"Hi, Lenox," I said, sitting down on my bed. "I wanted to call and thank you."

"You are very welcome. May I ask what happened?" The line was quiet.

I stood up. "What do you mean?" I asked, crossing to the window.

"Why you did that?"

Looking down onto the street below I saw the people gathering, their bodies lit up red and white from the car lights creeping by. Dinner was over and the party was just beginning.

"It's a bad habit," I answered.

"Freeing women from slavery?"

"It's my methodology I question."

"Ah, yes. It could have been more elegant."

I laughed.

"You have a very nice laugh, Sydney Rye."

The way he said my name seemed to zing through my body. "Thanks," I croaked. I grabbed a bottle of water out of the fridge and cracked it open.

"Would you like me to make love to you?" he asked, his voice promising something entirely different from love.

I drank the water, took a breath. He waited patiently. "Sorry," I said. "I'm not used to being propositioned on the phone."

"Do you like it?"

"Hmm, okay."

"I think you do."

He was right. I did.

"I'm not gonna go for that right now," I said, putting down the water and walking back to the window. "But, let me be very honest with you, since you've been so blunt yourself. I may very well be into that at a later date. But for now, can I just ask you a couple of questions?"

"Yes," was all he said, but I felt it right down to my toes.

"Great," I walked back to my water. "Malina said the two goons weren't talking. I imagine whoever they work for wants to know what happened."

"Several big men and three pit bulls," Lenox said. "That's who I heard attacked them. But to what they actually told their boss, I can't say for sure."

"And the women?"

"All safe. Living in a home with others who are also waiting for their asylum."

"Who did those guys work for?"

"You don't know?"

"No."

"You like danger?"

"It likes me."

"Hmm," he hummed against the phone. "His name is Ivan Zhovra. You've heard of him?"

"Yes, and he's looking for a bunch of guys with pit bulls?"

"From what I understand. But if you like danger, then he is just what you want."

"Tell me more about him."

I heard Lenox settle back into a leather chair, the material wheezing as he shifted his weight. The tinkle of ice cubes, a small sip, satisfied exhalation. "What do you want to know?"

"What would you want to know?"

"Ivan is ruthless and powerful. His followers are loyal, many of them new to this country. Ivan's only been in Miami for about five years. Threats, torture, tyranny are his tools. And he has used them to get to the top."

"The girls?"

"He moves them around the different clubs and then out of the city. That way they can't form any relationships. Even johns have sympathy."

"Do you think he has access to drugs? Something that wouldn't show up on a tox screen but could make a person black out and..." I paused trying to find the right words, "do something against their nature?"

The tinkle of ice again. "I've heard rumors."

"Yes?" I said, urging him to go on.

"Men blacking out after visiting their clubs. It's never the last place they were seen, often that's at an ATM, but they all forget and they all get robbed."

"What is it?"

"Possibly datura, they use it in Colombia mostly. It's rare here. I think it attracts attention from law enforcement and scares away customers."

"More than just your run of the mill sex slavery ring?"

"Exactly."

"Where does he get it from?"

"I don't know, like I said, it's just a rumor." I heard a voice behind him and his voice, away from the phone, respond in a foreign language. "I must go," he said. "Is there anything else you need to know?"

"No, thank you, you've been very helpful."

"It was a pleasure talking to you. Call anytime."

EK

When Mulberry and I arrived at Hugh's place the next day, Santiago opened the door and the smell of coconut oil and fresh baked bread wafted out of the apartment.

"Sydney!" Santiago said and gave me a generous hug. I discovered that he was the source of the coconut oil smell. Blue received a "Mi Amor" and a pet on the head. I introduced Santiago to Mulberry, who smiled a slightly confused smile.

Inside Hugh was at the stove stirring a pot. The smell of fresh herbs filled the kitchen. "I know it's not really Miami," Hugh said "but when I get depressed, I just like a good Soupe au Pistou with a hunk of homemade bread." Santiago slipped back into the kitchen at Hugh's side and I watched them work silently together, cutting bread, filling bowls, dolloping the paste of fresh herbs on top and then placing them on the dining table by the window. "I'm opening a bottle of rosé," Hugh announced. "Since, obviously, I'm not driving," he held out the monitor on his ankle as proof.

The rosé open, the bowls steaming, we sat down to an early lunch, passing around a bowl filled with crusty, just-out-of-the-oven bread. "So," Santiago said once we'd all had a moment to taste the food and wine and compliment the chefs. "I think I figured it out."

"What?" Mulberry asked.

"What happened to Hugh. I'm telling you, this happens all the time in Colombia, I just never heard of it used for murder before but," he shrugged, "the evil are always coming up with a new use for the Devil's Breath."

"It's also called scopolamine and datura, it has a lot of names," Hugh added.

I sipped my wine and stayed quiet.

"Sorry guys, you lost me," Mulberry said.

"In Colombia, where I am from," Santiago said, laying an elegant hand across his chest, "it is used to rob people. You blow it in their face, you know a poof," he placed his right hand, palm to chin, fingers extended straight out and blew a puff of air. "Or you put it under your nose," he wiped across his upper lip. "And then when you kiss someone they just, they lose their will and you can control them," he finished.

"Really?" I asked.

"Yes, it is quite common in Colombia."

Mulberry was nodding his head. "Yes, you're right. I saw a documentary about it a couple of years ago." He looked up at Santiago. "Thank you," he said. "I've got to make a call." He stood up from the table abandoning half a glass of wine and an almost empty bowl of soup.

Santiago beamed. "You think I'm right?" he asked me.

"Tell me more."

Santiago picked up his glass and held it as he spoke. "The criminals, they blow it in someone's face and then they take them to the ATM. They take them to their houses and make them show where all their valuables are hidden."

I thought of the blood spatter Edwards had pointed to, the evidence of someone else in the room. "So they go with them, to the ATM, to their houses."

"Yes, they go with you, to control you. My friend's grandmother, she had it done to her. She dropped on the floor. They gave her too much and she had a heart attack. It is very easy to kill accidentally with scopolamine."

Mulberry came back to the table "They're going to check Hugh's blood sample," he said.

"This could be good, very good," Santiago said. "If they can prove you were drugged and ordered to commit the crime, then how can they send you to jail?"

Mulberry frowned but didn't respond to the question. Instead he changed the subject. "Hugh, one of the things we wanted to ask you was what you know about Ivan Zhovra?"

Hugh shrugged and dipped a crust of bread into his soup. "Not much. He was a friend of Lawrence's. I really try to stay out of the front end of the business as much as possible."

"Oh, it's true," Santiago said. "He may be a big celebrity, but he does not like to act like it."

Hugh blushed. "I'm not a big celebrity. I understand that it's part of the job, but that's one of the reasons I liked working with Lawrence. He made nice."

"It looks like Lawrence owed Ivan a lot of money," I said.

Hugh didn't look surprised. "Gambling?" he asked. Mulberry nodded. Hugh sat back, abandoning his piece of bread floating in the soup, and looked out his window, the sun lighting his face, making him look a bit like a TV star. "I knew he gambled and I suspected he had a problem, but to be in debt to..."

"That's why he always comped Ivan when he came in," Mulberry suggested.

Hugh shrugged. "I didn't think to ask. We had a budget for that, whoever Lawrence thought should be comped was. It was considered a business expense, I guess."

"How closely did you watch the books?" Mulberry asked gently.

Hugh turned to him and frowned. "I really left it all to Lawrence."

"Did he take drugs?" I asked. "Lawrence, was he on pills, coke?"

Hugh shook his head. "I don't think he did coke anymore. Back in the day I'm sure, but he didn't party like that anymore. It was just gambling."

"I think he had an Ambien prescription," Santiago said. "But who doesn't?"

"What about selling drugs?"

"I don't think so," Hugh said. "But he wouldn't tell me."

Santiago was shaking his head. "He wasn't selling anything. No way would he bother with small stuff, and if he was moving weight then I doubt he'd have debt problems."

"Maybe," I said, and finished off my wine.

"We should probably get going," Mulberry said, standing. He picked up my empty bowl along with his. "I don't want to be drunk when I meet Ivan."

"He might be," Santiago said, following Mulberry into the kitchen with his and Hugh's bowls.

"Can I leave Blue here for a couple of hours?" I asked.

"Sure," Hugh said. He laughed. "Though I won't be able to walk him."

I laughed. "Don't worry about it. I shouldn't be long."

"What's up?"

"I just don't think I should take him to Ivan's."

"Why? You take him everywhere."

I looked over at the kitchen where Mulberry was washing dishes while Santiago dried. "I just think it's for the best in this situation."

Hugh shrugged. "You're the expert detective," he said with a smile before standing up. We grabbed the rest of the dishes and headed to help in the kitchen.

EK

On our way back to the car I asked, "Is there really a chance that if we find scopolamine in Hugh's system he'll be freed?"

Mulberry turned to look at me and shrugged. "That's a question for Edwards, but I'd say without the person who gave it to him, it's totally useless. Even with that I think the science may be hard to prove. I've never heard of a case where scopolamine was used as a defense. And a new defense is a pretty hard row to hoe."

"Right," I said. "Because the justice system is slow and resistant to change."

Mulberry laughed. "Yes, I suppose."

We climbed into the car and Mulberry started her up. 'Why did you leave Blue?" he asked.

"Well," I figured I had to tell him before we got to Ivan's. Mulberry had a right to know that it was possible I'd be recognized and we'd be attacked. I'd waited this long in the hopes that if we were already on our way he might not refuse to go in with me.

"You know when I was supposed to be shopping?"

"When you got your hair done?"

"You noticed."

Mulberry laughed. "I'm a detective."

"You didn't say anything."

"You are avoiding telling me something. Come on, spit it out, Rye."

"Fine. I beat up two of Ivan's men pretty bad."

"How bad?" Mulberry asked, keeping his eyes on the road.

"One got shot," I said. Mulberry glanced my way and then returned his gaze forward. "He shot himself," I clarified. "They were with three women and I could see what was going on."

"What do you mean?"

"Ligature marks, Mulberry. Those women were slaves."

"And where are they now?"

"Safe."

"I guess they got a pretty good look at you and Blue."

"Well, as you pointed out my hair is different." Mulberry snorted. "And I don't have Blue with me. Plus," I held up a finger, "I've got it on pretty good authority that they didn't want to admit their attacker was a woman so they said it was a group of men and several pit bulls."

"What authority?"

"I'm not at liberty to reveal my sources."

"Fine, let's just hope they're right."

"Another thing my source told me is there are rumors that datura is being used in Ivan's clubs."

"That's interesting," Mulberry said. "Just follow my lead, okay?"

"Don't I always?"

He laughed.

CHAPTER ELEVEN
DEMONS IN THE AFTERNOON

Mulberry held the door of the strip club open for me and I stepped in. For a moment, I stood on the threshold blinking into the space. It was dark, except for the slice of sunlight that cut around me casting my shadow a few feet into the room. The air was thick and still smelling of stale beer and the salty, sweet tang of pussy. "We aren't open yet," a woman said from inside.

I looked toward the voice as Mulberry stepped in next to me, letting the door swing shut, leaving us in a velvety darkness. As my eyes adjusted I saw there was a long formica bar down the left side of the room behind which was a single light glowing next to a computer screen. "I said we're not open," came the voice again. She was standing near the front of the bar, big bosom, thick arms, arched, plucked eyebrows above large brown eyes. Her dark hair pulled back into a pony tail. She wore a tight, white T-shirt that glowed a little in the dull light.

"Sorry to bother you," Mulberry said, starting toward her. "We are looking for Ivan Zhovra. Is he around?"

She leaned against the bar. "What's it to you?"

I followed Mulberry. To our right, tables and chairs sat around three individual stages. Thin silver poles reached down from the ceiling reflecting back the computer's light, appearing almost spectral. At the front of the room the main stage was shrouded in shadows. The walls were windowless and lined with booths made of a material that looked easy to clean. The floor was industrial indoor/outdoor carpeting.

Mulberry smiled at the hostile woman behind the bar and leaned toward her. I marveled at his transformation. He'd learned to use his sparkling hazel eyes instead of the threat of his broad shoulders. "I can see you're busy," Mulberry said, gesturing toward the pile of receipts next to the woman's computer. She pursed her lips and cocked her head. "But we really need to speak with Ivan. It's about Lawrence Taggert."

"That guy who got killed?"

Mulberry nodded and frowned. "I'm afraid so."

"What's that to Ivan?"

Mulberry shrugged. "That's what I'd like to talk to him about."

The woman stood tall, running her hand along the edge of the bar and shook her head. "He don't like cops."

I stepped forward. "Look," I said, sidling up next to Mulberry. "We're not cops," I smiled at her. "I mean really, do I look like a cop?"

She pursed her lips and narrowed her eyes, running them from the scar under my eye, down to loose T-Shirt and tight pants. She leaned back, crossing her arms. "No," she finally answered. "But he don't like to be disturbed."

"I suggest you go tell Ivan we're here. Tell him it's about Lawrence and see if he wants to talk to us."

She opened her mouth to speak and I slammed my fist on the bar. She jumped slightly, her eyebrows bouncing up. "I'm not going to ask you again." She recovered from her surprise and settled her face into a glare.

"I'll tell him. But he ain't gonna like your attitude."

"Yeah, I'll worry about that, you worry about delivering my message."

After she slinked through a back door, twitching her ample ass at us as she went, Mulberry turned to me. "Is that your bad cop?"

"I don't know, Mulberry, I was never a cop."

He turned around, putting his elbows on the bar behind him and leaning against it. "You woulda made one hell of an officer."

I laughed. "Yeah, because I'm *so* good with authority."

"Serpico baby," Mulberry said, and I laughed.

The sound of a door opening brought our attention back to behind the bar. A small white guy, balding, and wearing a sweatsuit that hung off his strong frame, looking comfortable and somehow slick, stepped into the room. Few men can wear sweats like that and this guy was one of them. He raised a lip in something between a snarl and a smile, showing off a gold tooth that caught the single lamp's yellow glow. A faded tattoo curled out from under the man's sweatshirt up his neck. More ink decorated his fingers, Cyrillic letters that meant nothing to me. "You vant to see Ivan?" he asked, his accent thick and voice gruff. "You threaten this bar? This woman?" he said, pointing to the big-breasted bartender who stood behind him, a look of satisfaction on her face.

Mulberry glanced at me and raised his brows in a *this is your show* look. "Yes," I answered him. "I want to see Ivan. I need to speak with him about an urgent matter and that woman," I pointed at her, "was making it difficult. I'm sure you can understand my frustration. Don't tell me you've never threatened anyone who stood in your way."

He raised his lip again, showing me the gold tooth and the twisted incisor next to it. "Vait."

The woman's face dropped as he pushed by her. She followed after giving me her best glare. It wasn't bad if you were trying to scare a kitten.

Moments later a giant of a man came out from the back but didn't approach us. His hair was short and blonde. He wore a shiny gray suit that didn't fit him nearly as well as his companion's velour matching set. The big man trained bright blue eyes on me. "You ask for me?" he said, not coming closer.

"Yes." I walked down the bar, approaching him. "I'm Sydney Rye and this is my partner Mulberry." I pointed toward Mulberry who followed close behind. "We are looking into Lawrence Taggert's murder and were hoping you'd be willing to speak with us."

He watched my approach, expressionless. "Looking into it for who?" Ivan's accent was slight only in comparison to the tattooed man's. It was obvious he came from somewhere cold, dark, with a Cyrillic alphabet.

Some part of the Soviet empire where men grew up hungry and rough. A place where generations bred the biggest, strongest, toughest people. The type that could survive every kind of torture Mother Nature threw at them from the frozen winters to muddy summers to the abject cruelty of man.

"We're not cops," I said.

He smiled. "So?"

"We know things about you."

He cocked his head. "So?"

"We might be able to help you."

"Help me?" he asked, his eyebrows raising. He frowned and shook his head.

"We know you had a relationship with Lawrence Taggert." I said.

He shrugged, his large shoulders rising against his thick neck, and frowned. "We were friends. This is known."

"I think we both know you were more than that."

The man smiled slowly. "What business is this of yours, little girl?"

Out of my peripheral vision I saw Mulberry's head turn to look at me, but I couldn't make out his expression. However, I could guess it was worried. Worried that I'd take a running leap at this mountain-size man, spring off the bar, and, placing one hand on his chin and the other at the top of his head, use my momentum to snap that tree trunk-size neck. But instead I smiled at him. "You're right Ivan, it is none of my business what you do or who you do it with."

I paused for a moment and looked around the dark bar, took a deep breath inhaling the stench of beer and sex. "But," I held up a finger and shook my hand gently, "I do have a very strong interest in who killed Lawrence Taggert and since you're clearly the absolute worst kind of scum on the earth, I'd say you're suspect #1." I held the hand still, my finger extended up.

Ivan stared at it for a moment and then burst out laughing. "You are very brave, little girl."

I smiled. "That's because I'm very strong."

"Come, we have a drink, we talk." He turned and headed toward the back of the bar.

"You are seriously lucky that worked," Mulberry whispered to me as we followed Ivan into the back room.

ЕК

Ivan led us into a small private office that smelled of cigar smoke and money. He offered us two chairs and took a third. His sweat-suited soldier stood behind him looking indestructible. A slight, blonde woman with pale skin wearing a short black mini dress came in and Ivan spoke to her in his native tongue. She listened, nodded, and left toward the bar.

"You drink," Ivan said. It wasn't a question. We nodded. "Smoke?" This time he was asking.

"No thanks," Mulberry said. Ivan's eyes fell on me. They were small for his face but bright blue. They looked like thick ice, cold and hard.

I shook my head. "Tell me about Taggert," I said.

Ivan turned to the man behind him and said something. The henchman nodded and then opened a cabinet, removing a dark wood humidor. He held it open in front of Ivan who looked at me. "Are you sure? They are the best."

I smiled. "Thanks, but I'm good."

Ivan shrugged and waved the box away. "I thought it was clear who killed Lawrence Taggert. Hugh Defry."

"You know him?"

"Of course," Ivan said. "I love his food, I will miss *Defry's*."

"You think Hugh was capable of something like this?"

Ivan held my gaze. "You must know what men are capable of."

"Why should I believe you didn't have him killed?"

Ivan held a hand to his chest as though I'd wounded him. "Why would I kill him?"

"Maybe he messed up?"

"How?"

I shrugged. The woman returned with three shots of clear liquid on a round tray. As she bent to offer me one I noticed fading bruises on her wrists. I took the drink and thanked her. She moved onto Mulberry who also took a glass. I checked her ankles and saw more marks. "I bet there are a lot of ways to mess up around here," I answered.

Ivan took a glass from the woman. "What makes you think it wasn't Hugh?" Ivan asked, holding his drink lightly in one hand.

"We're not at liberty to say," Mulberry answered.

Ivan smiled and looked at me. "You ask for information but you do not want to give any." I didn't answer. "If it was not Hugh, I would like to know who killed Lawrence. He was a valued business associate. There were things that he provided that no one else has. Maybe you can help me with this."

"In what way?" I asked.

Ivan shrugged again. "Maybe you can't. Salut," Ivan said, holding up the glass. Mulberry and I mimicked his movement and then we all took the shot. Strong, gasoline-like vodka hit the back of my throat but I kept my face still. Ivan watched me and smiled when I didn't cough or tear up.

"I tell you the truth. I did not kill Lawrence. You find out who did. I would very much like to know."

EK

As we got back in the car I paused for a moment and looked up at the strip club. The cinderblock building was painted with advertisements for the pleasures found inside. It looked grotesque in the bright mid-day sun. I thought about the bruises on that girl. She was probably undocumented, brought here for the express purpose of turning her into a prostitute. I wondered what her dreams had been, if she had any left.

My fingers tightened around the door handle as I thought about Ivan and his sweat-suited comrade. Men like that did not deserve to rule the world. Maybe Malina was right. Maybe we needed to do something. Then again, maybe that was just the lunch-hour drinking talking.

"You okay?" Mulberry asked.

I turned to him. "Yeah, just thinking." I took one last glance up at the building and then climbed into the car.

"Want to go back to the office and watch some surveillance video?" Mulberry asked.

"Sounds like a scream." Mulberry pulled onto the highway and we cruised along in silence for awhile. "What do you think Lawrence was doing for Ivan?" I asked. "I'd been thinking money laundering but I'm not sure. Didn't it sound like it wasn't that simple?" I asked Mulberry.

He changed lanes and exited. "Yeah," Mulberry said. "He seemed willing to do business until he realized we had no idea what he was talking about."

"Yeah."

"At least he didn't figure out you were the group of guys and pit bulls who just beat the shit out of his men."

"That's good," I agreed.

CHAPTER TWELVE
BIG BROTHER

"Hey," said Ashley, as we entered the viewing room, which was a floor beneath the conference room we'd been using. She swiveled in a black office chair, turning away from several screens that all showed the front entrance of *Defry*.

"How's it going?" Mulberry asked, taking a seat to her left. I sat in a matching chair on her right and Blue maneuvered himself under the desk with his snout resting on my foot. The room itself was small and dark. Four screens were set into the desk that Ashley worked at. Within arm's reach were a variety of dials and a keyboard color-coded for something I did not understand.

"I'm just going through the outdoor feed from the front of the restaurant for the day leading up to the fire."

"How far back have you watched?" I asked.

"So far," she leaned back in her chair and it seemed to sigh, "I've done the kitchen footage for three days prior to the fire. Nothing on that."

I smiled. "No evidence of someone sneaking in and sabotaging the oven?"

"Not as of yet," she smiled. "But, I'll go back further once I've gotten through this."

"Sydney, do you want me to set you up in a room to watch those gas station feeds?" Mulberry asked. I looked at the array of instruments in front of Ashley. Seeing my glance, Mulberry continued, "Don't worry, I'll show you the basics."

Mulberry took me to a room that was almost identical to the one where we'd found Ashley. He sat down in one of the dark leather chairs and pointed to another. I took my place and Blue curled up under the desk, happy to have a dark, quiet place to nap. Mulberry grabbed the armrest of my chair and pulled me close to his, right up in front of all the gadgetry. Knobs and keyboards, not my friends.

"Don't look so worried," he said with a smile. "You're gonna get this fine."

I shy away from technology. It is overwhelming and powerful. Without emotions there seems no angle at which to approach it.

Mulberry typed quickly onto the keyboard and a menu came up on one of the screens. He navigated to a file and clicked it, which caused it to open onto a different screen. A still, blurry image of the gas pumps at the Everglades station. He clicked another file and the next screen glowed to life, displaying an angle from inside the store, facing the cash register. Sanjit was leaning on his counter, looking out the door. Mulberry filled the next two screens with angles from different cameras. I could see the pumps, the register, the fridges filled with drinks that promised power, relief, and just plain sugar, as well as the bathroom door and aisle leading to it.

At the bottom of each screen a time clock paused at 9 pm, six months before the murder. "You want to start all the way back here?" Mulberry asked.

I laughed. "Can I start with the night of the murder and go backwards?"

"You can do anything you want with this thing," he said with a smile. He looked like a kid with a new video game as he turned back to the screen in the center of the console. He typed and explained what he was doing, but I wasn't listening. My eye had caught the way his lips and the whiskers of his stubble glowed in the computer's screen light and I was suddenly entranced, watching his mouth move as he spoke.

"Sydney," I realized he said my name.

"Hmm, yeah," I said, looking up at his eyes.

A smile teased the corners of his mouth. "You okay?"

"Yeah, I'm fine. Just um," I looked over at the screens. "How do I do it again?"

Mulberry laughed and turned back to the computer. "Here," he said. "See these knobs?" I nodded seeing the dials built into the desk. "They control the time on the four different monitors which you can see, obviously, from the clock on the bottom of the screen." He reached out and pointed at the time stamp. I nodded again. "If you want to go back or forward you just turn the corresponding knob."

He took one between his fingers and twisted it slowly. Action began to happen in the top left screen. Sanjit stood up from the counter and began to turn. When Mulberry stopped moving his fingers, so did Sanjit. "To jump faster you can go into your controls here," Mulberry brought up a window on the center screen, "and just type it in here." He showed me how each film was labeled and how to change the times. He turned to me. "Got it?"

I smiled but it was clear I had not got it. "Why don't you just watch with me?" I asked.

He leaned back in his chair and tilted his head, examining me. "Did you just ask for my help?"

"What?" I said with faux dismay.

"Sydney Rye asking for help." He folded his arms and looked smug.

"I don't like computers."

He laughed. "You know there is quite a bit of irony in that."

"What do you mean?"

"Because your legacy is being made on them."

I felt a chill run down my spine and land in my gut as a golf ball-size nut of anxiety. "What do you know about it?"

He leaned forward and put his hand on my knee. "I know about Joyful Justice," he said, his voice quiet and intimate.

"Do you think it's a good idea?" I asked, holding my breath, not sure I was ready to hear his answer. Scared of how deeply it might affect me.

Before he could respond the door opened. Ashley walked in and, seeing our intimate pose, flustered, apologized, and left quickly.

Mulberry and I both couldn't help but giggle. "I should probably go," Mulberry said as he stood. "Don't want the troops talking."

I furrowed my brow. "Who cares what she thinks?"

Mulberry looked down at me. "You would be wise not to ignore what other people say about you, Sydney. It can be dangerous to stay misinformed."

And with that he left, leaving me alone with the big bad computer.

EK

I figured out how to use the system easily enough. I started just turning the knobs and soon I was off, watching the daily life at the Everglades Quick n' Go. There was not much to see and plenty at the same time. I learned the schedule for the employees, who was late, who ate a lot of chocolate. I felt a bit like I was watching that Kevin Smith movie *Clerks*, but without any of the witty banter or cruel irony.

I watched the day that Hugh came from morning until night. The moment of truth, when Hugh's car pulled into view and stopped in front of pump #4, was a letdown after watching ten hours of the same thing happen in fast forward. I slowed down the tape, inching it along, making Hugh pump gas in a herky-jerky painfully slow way. I'd watched cars and drivers do the same thing all day.

On those hours of tape a car arrived, its driver climbed out, sometimes there were kids in the back, often at least a passenger. But at pump 4 it was hard to tell if there was anyone in the passenger seat unless they propped an elbow out the window, or decided to get out and take a stretch, pulling up shirts and exposing bellies to the camera they didn't realize was there.

But if anyone was with Hugh, if there was a puppet master sitting by his side, then he or she would know about the cameras and make sure not to be seen. With the tank nearly full the only reason to stop at this station was to make sure this footage happened. I stared at the dark passenger window of Hugh's car as he replaced the nozzle and inched back to the driver's side. Leaning across the desk, slowing the action and pushing closer to the screen, I tried to decipher some movement, some hint of life from the dark pixels that filled the car's interior.

The sedan began to move, the overhead fluorescents glinting off the glass. It pulled into the darkness of the Everglades, its taillights receding in the gloom. I sat back and stared at the screen, allowing it to return to normal speed.

The footage from that night became slowly stiller until the headlights that had passed by in a semi-regular flow fully stopped for two hours. I marveled that Sanjit kept his place open for such long hours when so few customers were passing by. As the sun rose on the day that Hugh was arrested, the footage stopped. It was the end of what he'd given me.

I went to the main screen, put in midnight from two days before the murder and hit play. It worked. All four cameras began at the same place. I was quietly pleased with myself for figuring it out. Sure, Mulberry showed it to me like an hour ago but still, not every day I managed something new on a computer. And then Mulberry was back in my mind, swirling around, balling all my emotions into a big fat mess.

Blue sensed my tension and sat up, pushing against me, his wet nose touching my hand. I looked down at him and held his steady gaze. Staring deep into his mismatched eyes I found some peace. "What are we gonna do, boy?" I asked him. He blinked and settled his head across my lap. My cell phone pinged, and I looked down at a message from Dan. *Found some really interesting stuff about datura, can you meet for dinner, 8?*

How did he find out about the datura? Joyful Justice at work? Were Santiago and Hugh members of Joyful Justice too? How many members were there? I thought about Mulberry's warning and glanced up at the screens. "I should really go on that site," I said to Blue. He sighed and closed his eyes. I needed to figure out what happened to Hugh before anything else. I returned Dan's message telling him to text me the address of the restaurant.

I spent another two hours going over uneventful footage from those two final days when there was a knock at the door. "Yup," I said, hitting the pause button like a regular pro.

"Hey," Mulberry said, Ashley standing right behind him. "We're going to get take out. You want?"

"Wait, what time is it?" I checked my phone and saw I was about to be late to meet Dan. "I can't. I've got to run," I said, standing up and grabbing my bag. Blue came out from under the desk and stretched out his front paws, lifted his tail in the air and yawned as he fanned it lazily back and forth.

"Looks like he had a good nap," Mulberry said, smiling down at him.

"I'll call you later," I told him as I pushed past and hurried down the hall.

He caught up to me at the elevators. "Hey," he said. "What's going on? Where are you going?"

"I'm meeting Dan."

He smiled but looked annoyed. "Fine, enjoy your dinner," he said, an edge to his voice. Then he quickly turned back toward Ashley who waited at the end of the hall pretending not to watch us.

EK

I pulled up to the restaurant only ten minutes late and Dan smiled as he watched me approach in a hurry. "Sorry," I said as I joined him at the outdoor table.

"No problem, I'm used to you being late," he said it as though my tardiness was charming.

"I'm not always late," I said.

"Sure, if you're on Indian time I'd say you're more than punctual."

I laughed. "Yeah, right, maybe I'm judging myself by the wrong standards."

"Hey, you're here and that's what matters," Dan said as he picked up the menu. "Want me to order?" he asked.

"Please." Dan always picked the best stuff, and I'd learned that if I didn't have him order for me I'd just be jealous of his choice. The waiter came over and Dan greeted him in Spanish, then ordered several dishes I'd never heard of.

"This is your first time in a Cuban restaurant?" the waiter said, turning to me.

I looked over at Dan and then back to him. The waiter was round in the middle wearing high pants with a white button-down shirt tucked in. "Yes," I answered.

"Ah, then I will make something special for you. For your special lady, eh, Dan."

"You guys know each other?" I asked.

"Sure," the waiter answered. "He is one of my favorite customers."

I smiled at him and he laughed. "I leave you two lovebirds alone, eh."

"Lovebirds?" I said to Dan after the waiter left us.

Dan shrugged. "He made an assumption."

"Why?" I asked. "Did you used to bring a lot of dates here?"

He blushed. "Maybe one or two."

"Dan!"

"What? I'm not trying to date you, Sydney, I just really like the food."

"Fine," I said.

He laughed.

"So," I said, changing the subject, "what did you find out?"

Dan sat forward. "A lot. Datura is fascinating. You know, I'd heard about it before, but now that I've dug deeper, this shit is crazy."

"Yeah?" I said, leaning toward him. The waiter arrived with a mojito for me, and I thanked him before turning back to Dan.

"It's used a lot in Colombia for robbing people, raping women, the list goes on. Now, I didn't find any cold hard examples of people being forced to commit murder while on the drug, but it seems like it could be done. There is some new stuff hitting the streets now, just in the past six months or so, they are calling designer."

"What do you mean?"

"Before this new shit it was basically the ground-up seeds of the datura plant that they transformed into a powder using a method similar to turning coco leaves into cocaine. That's a pretty basic drug, unlike ecstasy or molly which are both a mix of stuff that makes you feel a variety of ways. You can buy "up" ecstasy or "down" ecstasy and each version will work on you differently. Now someone is doing it with datura. Only instead of "up" or "down", it's how long it lasts, how compliant the victim is, how much they remember, how horrific the hallucinations."

"Wow," I sat back and sipped at my mojito. "So who is selling it and who is buying it?"

"Mostly it's in Colombia. I should know more about Miami soon."

"There are rumors that Ivan Zhovra is giving it to his girls."

"I've heard that."

The waiter arrived with our food and we ordered another round of drinks.

EK

When I woke up the next morning I could feel that first mojito and its three siblings sitting on my forehead laughing at me. Blue noticed I was awake and jumped off the bed ready for our morning jog. "Not today," I muttered, before rolling myself back up in the blankets. Blue warbled at me, ending his protest with a high pitched whine. "Shut up," I said, but Blue came around to my face and pushed his wet nose into the covers until he found my eye and then licked. "Ew," I said and rolled away from him again.

He barked once, short and high pitched. "Ah, Jesus, fine," I said, throwing the covers aside. Blue pranced around me as I made my way to the bathroom. He tried to follow me in but I closed the door, leaving him to wait while I brushed my teeth and made myself somewhat presentable to the world. I drank a big glass of water, gulping it down like medicine, then walked back out into the room.

Blue pranced around me, occasionally letting out a small warble of excitement as I dressed. Finally, shoes tied, sunglasses on, hat low, I left the room and headed down to the beach. Instead of staying on the path, I cut over to the sand and slipped out of my sneakers, leaving them hidden in some of the foliage that grew from the dunes before heading out barefoot onto the beach. It was early enough that the sand did not burn my feet but I jogged toward the water anyway. The ground was surer by the waves, more compact, better for running. Blue jumped into the sea as I ran parallel to it. The warm waves washed over my toes with each undulation. Wet, Blue ran to my side. I tapped my left hip and he moved to that side, then my right. Gentle, persistent training was important for both of us.

The sun was still just above the horizon as we passed several young men, tan and wearing white shorts. They pulled out chaises for the customers who were sure to arrive. Between the beach club operations, large swaths of empty beach greeted me, only the occasional early-bird family setting up their site, preparing for the sun to beam more fully down on them.

We ran until the sun reached my shoulder and slanted across the sand, casting our long shadows up toward the dunes. I turned us around. We settled into an easy, loping jog, a pace I felt I could maintain forever. But then the music in my headphones changed and the beat seemed to speak directly to my feet. I felt the wave of it, the force of the sounds pushing me forward faster. And soon, Blue and I were sprinting, running as fast as I could, legs extended, arms pumping, mouth open and pulling air between my teeth in raspy whooshes that couldn't go on for long. The beat played on but I slowed, my heart racing, legs burning, feet feeling fully polished.

EK

Heading back to the viewing room, I walked past a secretary who offered me coffee. I agreed and she brought it into the room as I queued up my footage. "Mr. Maxim would like to see you, is now a good time?" she asked as she placed my coffee on the desk.

"Sure." I began to stand up and head for the door but she stopped me.

"Mr. Maxim is going to come to you."

"He is?"

She nodded, looking as confused as me.

Fifteen minutes later he showed up. I was watching the "same but different" footage of the gas station, starting to recognize the commuters and notice similarities among the tourists. He knocked but didn't wait for an invitation to enter. "Hi," I said, pausing the footage and turning my chair to the door.

He smiled and took a seat on the couch that lined the back wall. "Good to see you," he said. In the muted light he looked nicer somehow. The sharpness of his jaw, the glint in his eyes all seemed softened. I nodded, not wanting to encourage him. He shouldn't think I wanted to see him because I didn't. And yet, I'd waited for his arrival with impatience in my gut and a spark of excitement in my breast.

"How are you liking it?" he asked, gesturing toward the computer in front of me.

"I'm learning to use it," I answered.

He nodded. "How sure are you he didn't do it?"

"Did Mulberry tell you about the datura idea?"

"Yes, he briefed me yesterday. It's interesting."

"If we find it in his blood sample, will that be enough evidence?" I felt silly asking the question, like a kid who wants something to be true but knows it isn't. I knew that simple evidence of drugs was not a defense, especially a defense never tried before. It was very possible, I realized in that moment, that even if I did everything right, even if we gathered every shred of evidence and proved that Hugh was not in his right mind when he committed the murder, it still might not be enough.

Bobby didn't answer for a moment. He just stared at me, watching the thoughts crossing my face. "You know the answer to your question and that's why I'm wondering if he would prefer to run?"

"What?"

"We could get him a new identity. Do you think he is very attached to his life here? Would he go?"

"Not without a fight," I answered him.

"In time we will see what we can do. I promise to use every power I have to keep him free, but, Sydney, there is only so much I can do."

I laughed. "I don't believe you."

He smiled. "I like that you have faith in my abilities."

"Yeah, well, I've never doubted those."

He sat forward. "Are you liking it here in Miami, the car, it's good?"

I sat back, made uneasy by his earnest tone. "Yes," I couldn't keep a smile from drifting onto my lips as I thought about the car. Bobby nodded in silent agreement.

"I hope you like it here, Sydney. I hope that you stay."

"In Miami. I don't know." I said, surprised that I didn't just throw the offer back in his face.

"You can live wherever you want. You can do whatever you want. As long as we're on the same side."

"Same side," I said, pulling a knee up to my chest. "That's an interesting idea."

Bobby looked down at his watch. "We can talk more soon. Dinner tonight perhaps."

"I'm busy," I said. "Working." I pointed at the machine before me.

Bobby smiled. "Perhaps I'll stop in later then."

Two hours later I was bored out of my mind. To alleviate the boredom I decided to double check Ashley's work. She said she'd watched the kitchen footage from the night of the fire for three days prior, and I believed her. I just wanted to see it for myself. I called the secretary and had her switch the files for me. It looked simple enough and I thought I'd be able to get back to it on my own.

I started with dinner service the night before the fire. Unfortunately, the angle in the kitchen covered up the oven in question so it was impossible to know if someone had cleaned it or not; it also meant that someone could have sabotaged it without being seen. The only angle in the kitchen was from the far side of the service bar where the waiters picked up their dishes.

I watched the prep work, admiring again the way that Hugh and Santiago moved together in the kitchen. Even as the speed picked up there was very little tension. Though it was silent I could see Santiago calling out the orders as each one popped up from his printer and then turning back to his stovetop. Hugh worked rapidly, moving from one station to the next, hardly speaking to his staff who seemed to know what to do without his interruption. Often he took a small spoon and tasted from the pots and saucepans that bubbled and steamed on the stove top. Before each plate went out he reviewed it and then placed it on the metal, shoulder-height shelf. I saw his hand come down soundlessly onto a small bell over and over again.

It was strange to watch the kitchen crew in black and white, silent, like a 1920's film. How much had changed since those first flickering films that captured the imagination of a species.

The orders slowed and the crew began to clean up. With the last dishes out and the kitchen cleaned, the team opened beers and laughed, enjoying their end-of-shift drink. I sped up the tape, watching them all leave in quick, jerky steps, the lights went out and darkness fell upon the screen.

I sped through the darkness until the lights flicked back on and the routine I'd watched the day before repeated itself. Right as dinner service was about to begin in earnest, someone off camera called the crew out of the kitchen. As the last one came around the counter the screen went black. The explosion tripped the electric. The fire investigators and insurance investigators had looked at these tapes. They agreed the trap just wasn't cleaned enough.

I switched to the footage from the front of the restaurant provided by one of the city's webcams. It was in color and stuttered occasionally. I pulled a knee up to my chest and hugged it as I fast forwarded through the days, looking for something to click; for a clue to present itself to me.

At around noon the secretary knocked on my door and offered me lunch, but I waved her away, my mind and body consumed with the task at hand. After going back a week, I went back another. Lawrence hardly showed up on the kitchen tapes and it became clear that he spent his time in the front of the house. There was no indoor video, but I saw him come and go at least a couple of nights a week. Always greeting his guests at the door. They ranged in age, gender, and physical beauty, but they all had one simple little thing in common. Money. They all looked like money.

His wife, who only showed up once in the weeks I watched, looked most like money of them all. In the grainy footage she appeared ageless, her figure lithe, posture proud, outfit flawless. She seemed intensely subtle next to her TV-personality of a husband.

Ivan came often. He brought a group with him every time. The women were always different, the men almost always the same. He entered the place like he owned it. Kissing the hostess on the cheek and stopping among the outside tables to shake hands and laugh.

If Taggert was at the restaurant they sat together, often in a corner booth by the window. I could just make them out through the sidewalk tables, umbrellas, and patrons. I could see them talking calmly. Then as the wine bottles came and went they would slowly get drunk, the stiffness of Ivan's lines melting a little. By the time the brandy landed on the table, Ivan's big hands would be pawing the woman closest to him. Taggert comfortable and smiling, watching the show. The woman's face was almost always obscured.

I rewatched the footage from the night of the fire repeatedly. While I could not hear the explosion, the moment was obvious. A woman in a short skirt who was walking by the restaurant jumped and her mouth opened in a silent scream. The man walking next to her moved his body to protect her.

In the front row of tables a group of four men in suits all held their cocktails loosely, their bodies relaxed. Then they lurched to the ground, dropping their glasses, two of which broke, the third rolling down the sidewalk, dumping ice and booze as it spun. Closer to the door, two women, dressed for fun in high heels and tight jeans, got up and ran, their postures mimicking frightened horses. Head back, neck long, heels stuttering, they pushed past the tables to get out to the street.

Then I saw him, he was dining alone and his face was obscured by an umbrella stand but when everyone else jumped, he didn't. The man didn't even flinch. I leaned forward, biting down hard on my bottom lip, and moved the footage one click at a time, waiting for him to reveal himself. But he never did. Soon after the explosion, when the crowds began to pour out of the restaurant, smoke following them in a billow of gray, he left, hidden from sight by the crowd of scared pedestrians.

I backed up the footage, figuring I'd find him when he arrived but the man climbed out of a cab directly in front of the restaurant, never turning his face toward the camera. Was this the guy? The puppeteer? Or was I just grasping at straws?

I watched him take his seat, a low hat blocking his face as he turned, repositioning the umbrella pole between the camera and himself. A white guy about average height, dressed in a button-down shirt and dark pants, his sleeves rolled up to combat the dying heat of the day. Dark hair peeked from beneath his hat.

What did that get me? Looking for a puppeteer, average height and weight with dark hair. Should I put an ad in the classifieds? I laughed aloud at the idea and that's when I realized I needed a break.

CHAPTER THIRTEEN
UNHELPFUL BOTANISTS

Blue and I went down to the lobby and out onto the street. It was hot and a breeze blew down the block, seeming to pick up speed as it rushed between the tall buildings. It was late afternoon, the sun tilted toward the west side of the world. Traffic was beginning to clog the narrow streets as rush hour began. A Lamborghini, yellow and absurd, revved its engine and then shot off down the block, braking hard at the next red light.

I'd neglected to leash Blue and he wandered down the block, sniffing at trees and tires. I followed him, letting my mind wander over the image of the man in the hat. My phone rang and I saw Dan was on the line. "Hey," I said, watching Blue as a mother pushed a stroller by him. She eyed him but didn't look nervous.

"Hey," Dan said. He sounded excited. "I found out that a world-renowned expert on datura teaches at Sloan University right here in Miami."

"Really?" Blue looked up at the tone of my voice and pricked his ears.

"Yes, I was going to head over there tomorrow and see if I could talk to him. Want to come?"

"Yes," I answered. "Where should I meet you?"

Traffic was light when I left for the university the next afternoon. During the twenty minute drive I thought over the tapes I'd rewatched, seeing a ton of people who could have been the guy, the one who didn't flinch, but I had no way of knowing. He was just too nondescript.

I parked in the school's visitors lot. It was a small institution from what I could tell, housed in a complex of low-rise buildings with palm trees and paved paths. Blue and I started toward a board with a map on it when I heard Dan call my name. "Hey," he said as he crossed the parking lot towards us. He looked down at my car. "Nice ride," he said. "Where'd you get that?"

"It's a loaner," I answered.

Dan let it go and we started toward the botanical building. Dan held the door for me and we walked into a carpeted hallway, the air cold, the lights fluorescent. Everything about it cried institution and it made my skin itch. The first door to our right was open, a plaque next to the entrance announced it as the office. The young woman sitting behind the desk smiled. Her medium-length brown hair was pulled back into a pony tail. She wore a sweater over a matching top. I believe that's called a sweater set, I told myself as we approached her. "Hi," she said, "how can I help?"

Dan smiled at her and asked about seeing the professor. On the counter were several pamphlets about the courses offered there. I picked one up and scanned down the list of classes. It might as well have been in Latin. Then I realized it was in Spanish and felt like kind of an idiot. I put it back and was about to return my attention to Dan and the girl behind the counter when I saw a pamphlet for a "Semester in the Swamp." I picked it up and opened the front flap when I realized Dan was talking to me. "Sydney, that works for you?"

"Whatever you think is best," I said. Dan smiled and nodded, a note of amusement in his eyes.

The girl came around the corner and led us down the hall. She looked over her shoulder and smiled at Dan before opening a door and motioning for us to enter. We walked into a lab room. Two students wearing white coats looked up from microscopes. "Here you go," she said. "Professor Nablestone will be here soon. This is his next class."

Dan thanked her and she left. The two students, a girl with short blonde hair and a boy whose skin was so black it glowed almost purple, watched us. "Hi," Dan said, moving down the aisle between the large black lab tables, each with its own sink. "You guys the TAs?"

They both nodded and then the boy spoke. "Yes," he said, a slight accent on it that made it sound musical.

"You work on research with the professor?" Dan asked.

"Yes, can I help you with something?" He sat back on his stool, leaning away from the microscope.

Dan smiled. "That's nice of you. We're doing some research for a case we're working on. We're private investigators and we suspect that one of our clients has been drugged with datura."

The man's brow furrowed. "I see."

"Well," the girl said, "that's something the professor has written about extensively."

"Yes," I smiled. "That's why we're here."

She looked over at me. Her eyes were light brown under eyebrows plucked almost into non-existence. "He's widely published. Anything he hasn't published he's not going to want to tell you."

Dan cleared his throat. "Really, we're just looking for basic knowledge."

"Then I wouldn't waste the professor's time. Read his work," she said.

And with that she returned her attention to the microscope in front of her. I looked over at the boy. "I'm Sydney, by the way," I said, extending my hand as I stepped up to him. He shook it politely, his hand was rough with callouses. "You do a lot of gardening?" I asked.

"I'm a botanist," he answered and, again, I felt a bit like an idiot. Kind of an "I carried a watermelon" moment.

"This is Dan," I said, moving on, "and Blue."

"I was not aware they allowed dogs in the classrooms," the girl spoke up again.

"Aja," the man said, extending his hand to Dan, who shook it. "I'm interested, what makes you think your client was drugged with datura, specifically?"

"He tested positive for it," I answered. A sort of lie.

Aja's eyes narrowed. "Tested positive for what exactly?"

"We're not scientists," Dan said. "We just want to know what kind of effect it can have on people, to see if it fits with our case."

Blue touched my hip and I heard voices and footfalls filling the halls. The door behind us opened and students began to enter. The girls wore either pajama pants and UGG boots or coochie cutters and wife beaters. The boys wore the male equivalent (pajama pants with flip flops or khaki shorts and button-down shirt). With them rich and varied smells—perfume, shampoo, body odor, pheromones. Aja stood up and headed to the front of the class. "Excuse me," he said.

"Let's wait outside," I suggested.

Dan agreed and we returned to the hallway, now bustling with students and teachers moving between classes. I stood close to the wall and concentrated on making myself invisible. Allowing my eyes to pass over people, seeing without seeing. An older man, his hair thinning on top, wearing a button-down shirt tucked into crisp blue slacks, sauntered toward our doorway. "Excuse me," I said as he went to enter. "Are you Professor Nablestone?"

A look of annoyance flurried over his face. "Yes," he answered. "And I am busy."

"Sorry to bother you, but my name is Sydney Rye and I'm a private investigator." His expression remained annoyed. "I think that one of my clients has been drugged with datura, and I wanted to talk to you."

He looked through the glass on the door at the almost full room. "I'm sorry but I don't have time. Anything you need to learn can be found in my writings. Read them and if you still have questions, email me." He pulled out his wallet and removed a white card from one of the pockets. Dan took the card and the professor brushed past us into his classroom.

"Friendly bunch," I said. Dan laughed.

We started back toward the exit and I pulled out the pamphlet I'd picked up in the office. "Check this out," I said, handing it over to Dan. He took the pamphlet from me. "Look at the map."

He opened up the "Semester in the Swamp" pamphlet. "It's not far from where Lawrence Taggert's body was found."

"That's what I thought."

We pushed through the doors back into the bright day. As Dan headed to his car, Blue jumped into the Audi and I climbed in after him. It was hot in the car and I lowered the windows and blasted the air. As I was about to pull out, I saw a girl with blonde hair, the rude TA of Professor Nablestone, push through the doors into the sunlight. She squinted and lowered her head, pulling out a pair of sunglasses from her lab coat pocket. Her hair was so blonde it reflected almost silver in the sunlight. I watched her go over to a tan Volvo that had seen better days. It looked like it was from up north and had gone through a couple of winters before moving to the sunshine state. The girl opened the back door, reached in, and pulled out a bag before pushing the door closed with her hip and heading back into the building. The Volvo was old enough that she had to use her key to lock it.

I stared at the car for a couple more minutes. Next to it was a Jaguar, a classic, when the shape still made you think of a jungle cat. It was forest green with tan leather interior, its chrome almost blinding in the bright day. I was pretty sure I recognized both those cars from the gas station tapes. Picking up my phone I called Dan. "What's up?" he asked.

"Follow me back to FGI. I think I have something."

EK

Dan met me at the FGI building, but when we went to pass through security they would not let Dan come up. "He's my guest," I said.

The man behind the desk didn't smile. "You don't have clearance to have a guest," he explained.

"Clearance? Fine, can you call Robert Maxim's office for me please?"

He picked up the phone. "I have a Ms. Rye down here, she wants to speak to Mr. Maxim about guest privileges." He listened for a moment and then replaced the handset. "Mr. Maxim is in a meeting. He has time at 6 pm to discuss the matter."

I bit down on my bottom lip trying to control my anger. I did not like being told what I could and could not do. I wanted to call Mulberry, but I didn't want to end up yelling into the phone while standing under the watchful eyes and many lenses of FGI. "Fine," I said to the security officer. "I'll come back."

"We're taking my car," I said to Dan as we headed back toward the parking lot.

"Where we going?"

"I'm not sure."

EK

I pulled out of the parking lot at a speed that made my tires screech, but the wheel stayed steady in my hand and the car safely on the road. Dan didn't say anything as I found the entrance to the highway and entered, headed south. "You okay?" he asked as we swerved between cars. I took the turns tight, the spaces between the lanes frustrating since I couldn't fit through them. It made me miss my motorcycle.

"I'm fine," I said breaking hard, dipping in behind a truck, then swerving across two lanes of traffic to exit onto 8th Street. Dan braced himself against the doorframe and the arm rest, Blue stayed low, stretched across the back seat, his tail up in the air helping him stay balanced. "Sorry," I said as I slowed to a red light. "I just need—" I didn't finish my sentence as the light turned green and I shot us forward, zooming west toward the Everglades. Only ten minutes of McDonalds and big box stores before I hit the casino and then disappear past it into the forever landscape of the Everglades. I felt that there was something there. Somewhere in the depths of that swamp was information that I needed. I just had no idea what it was.

"Okay," Dan said. He sat back against the seat.

I saw the sign for the casino up ahead, the last building that rose taller than the apple trees. We zoomed past it, hitting the green light and continued into the swamp. I looked in my rearview mirror at the city behind us, glimmering in the dying sunlight of the day. It felt good to be free of it. Free of its cruel plastic surface, its deeply dark inner workings. The Everglades felt safe to me compared to that environment.

I pulled over into the gas station and Dan looked over at me. "This is where Hugh stopped?"

I nodded. "Do you have a picture of the professor?"

"I can bring one up on my phone."

"Perfect. What about his blonde assistant?"

Dan shrugged. "Maybe. Any idea what her name was?"

I shook my head.

"No worries, I can probably track her through Aja if he's got a Facebook profile."

I climbed out of the car as Dan began to search and opened the back door for Blue, who leapt onto the cracked pavement, took a shake and then a deep stretch before wandering to where short cropped grass pushed up through the gas station parking lot. I looked past him to the far side of the canal. Grasses swayed in the breeze, golden and purple and pink depending on which way they bent. But never the same bright green as the grass that Blue was now peeing on. Well, that grass was gonna be bronze soon.

Dan got out of the car and held up his phone. "Ready."

We went into the shop, our entrance announced by an electric tone. Sanjit was behind the counter. "Hi," I said. He brightened when he recognized me.

"How are you? I hope your case is becoming successful."

"Thanks. I was wondering if you had ever seen this guy?"

Dan held the phone out to him and Sanjit took it in his hands. "Yes, I think so." He tilted his head back and forth in that oh-so-familiar Indian gesture.

"Do you know his name?"

Sanjit shook his head. "He is not very friendly."

I laughed. "My thoughts exactly."

Dan held his hand out for the phone and Sanjit returned it. Dan messed with it for a moment and then handed it back to Sanjit. "What about these two?" he asked, handing the phone over again. I caught a glimpse of Aja and the woman sitting together at what looked like some kind of gala, he in a suit, she in a simple black dress.

Sanjit nodded. "She comes quite often and him, too." His head shook side to side again. "They are not very friendly either but at least they say hello." He looked at the photo for a moment longer. "Her schedule is very diligent," he said, handing back the phone.

"What do you mean?"

"She is here every Wednesday, Thursday, and Friday at noon, buys a bottle of water and a Cliff bar, always the peanut butter flavor. Then she returns at 8 and gets another water and chocolate chip Cliff Bar."

"Do you know where they work?"

Sanjit shrugged. "No, they all work together?"

"Yes," I answered. "At the research facility down the road."

Sanjit frown. "The university? I didn't think that ever opened. There is no sign."

Back in the car I pushed past 80 as we raced west into the Everglades. The sky lit up like a neon peach pie as the sun dropped lower. It touched the horizon, which seemed somehow not that far away, just over there on the other side of those grasses. I felt that if I just stayed on that road, flat and steady, I'd get there.

"Don't you think it's strange that the Research Center wouldn't have a sign?" Dan said. "The Univeristy was full of students."

"Yes, it's very weird," I said.

"Where are we going?" Dan asked.

"I'm just driving," I admitted. "No destination in mind."

"Want to get a bite?" he asked. I looked over at Dan, the pink of the sunset making him glow. "Look, there."

I followed his finger down the road and saw a long shack coming up on our right. I slowed down as we approached the structure. It didn't have a parking lot, just a bit of gravel spread out in the grass. It was a big dip down to reach the open air dining hall, and I enjoyed navigating the sports car at the sharp angle.

Big-bulbed, multi-colored Christmas lights draped across the restaurant's roof. The *open* sign was red neon and hung at a slight angle. A woman in her early 50s leaned against one of the posts, her strawberry blonde hair piled on her head. She wore a pair of shorts, pleated in the front, and a worn sweatshirt. The woman smiled at us as we climbed out of the car. "Picked a pretty time to show up," she said.

And she was right, it was as if the whole landscape was shrouded in some kind of pink shimmering gauze; there were no hard edges, deep shadows, or bright spots. Everything was muted except the western sky. At the horizon, where the sun grazed the distant grasses it was bright orange and hot pink. Where we stood, as well as along the dock that lined the restaurant, the light seemed safe and mellow.

We ordered gator bites, burgers with fries, and beers. Sandy, who introduced herself as the "owner operator" of Everglades Eatery, brought our drinks and then settled in at the bar to watch the news on mute. Dan and I sat on the same side of the table, watching the final moments of the day fade away. The brilliance at the horizon vanished in an instant, leaving twilight covering the land.

We'd finished our beers before the darkness really started to sink in. It came from within the grass, starting between the blades. It gathered in the apple tree hammocks, and crept between their trunks, into the water, and across the sky. The clouds that made the sunset so spectacular now blocked the stars.

We paid the bill and got back to my car. As we headed back toward the city, its lights reflected off the low cloud cover filling the eastern horizon with an eerie red glow. Lightning flashed in the clouds but it was too far for the sound of thunder to reach us.

When I dropped Dan off at his car he asked where I was going. "I need to see Bobby," I answered.

Dan nodded. "I'll see you tomorrow," he said, and leaned in for a hug. I reached around his shoulders and his arms wrapped around my waist. I pushed up on my tip toes and he bent down so that we fit together, our necks intertwined. A quick kiss on my shoulder and Dan released me.

CHAPTER FOURTEEN
BULLETS AND BANTER

I went back to the security desk. The guard from earlier was replaced with a guy who shared none of the same facial features but still managed to wear the exact same expression of disinterest and disgust. "Please let Bobby Maxim know Sydney Rye is here to see him."

"He is expecting you." The man stood up and motioned for me to step through the turnstile. Blue and I followed him around the corner and to a single elevator door. He pressed the call button and the doors opened. Pulling out a key, he walked into the elevator and turned a lock where buttons would normally be. He motioned for me to step aboard, removed his key, and left. The door closed silently between us and the box began to rise. There was no way of knowing how many floors we passed. This was an express.

The elevator glided to a stop and the doors slid open. Blue and I walked out into a windowless foyer paneled with dark and caramel-hued wood. At the center of the parquet floor was a marble topped table with a white orchid on it. Beyond the table a door opened. A woman with gray hair swept into an updo nodded at me. She smiled and her blue eyes lit up with friendliness. "Mr. Maxim will see you now. Please come in."

Blue and I walked around the table, his nails clicking musically on the fine wood, and through the door. It appeared to be the secretary's office. To one side was a desk, behind it floor-to-ceiling windows that looked out over the bay, Miami Beach, and the ocean beyond. A nearly full moon shone between two clouds and lit the ocean up in tiger stripes of dazzling light. To our right was a waiting area with thick carpeting and sleek furniture, the walls the same deep brown wood as the foyer.

Robert's assistant walked past me and toward another door, this one padded and upholstered in leather and decorated with brass studs. She pulled the door wide and motioned for me to step through.

Looking through the opening past the beckoning woman, all I could see of the room beyond was part of an Oriental rug and bookshelves. I tilted my chin up and walked through, Blue's warmth at my hip. "Sydney, glad you could make it," Bobby said. He was sitting behind a large wooden desk to my left. He stood. "Please, have a seat," he motioned toward one of the two leather chairs that faced his desk. I crossed the room, noticing the height of the bookshelves and the massiveness of the space.

I sat down and crossed my legs. Blue sat by my side. "You want to talk about having visitors?" He sat across from me, unbuttoning his jacket as he did. Bobby was wearing a blue shirt, no tie, and a fitted jacket. With the silver hair at his temples and understated watch, it came off as powerful and sleek.

"I just want to have an understanding of what's going on right now."

Bobby steepled his fingers. "So like a woman to want to define our relationship," he said with a smile. "Do you ever play chess?"

"No."

"Ah, you should learn. It would be quite good for you. And I have a feeling you'd be good at it."

"Are you?"

He smiled. "The best." He leaned back. "Let me ask you this, Sydney. What do you see as your role? Lord knows it's not as my employee. Are you my client perhaps?" He held up a hand. "No, that would be Hugh. So," he tapped an elegant finger against his chin.

"I'm helping with the investigation."

"Ah, yes, I'll agree to that, but in what capacity? How do I fit you into the books?"

"Why do you need a record?"

"That's the whole thing. Let's say I let you come up here, into FGI headquarters, with a guest, who then does something to our computer system. How do I explain what happened?"

"You think I'm going to sabotage you?"

Bobby smiled. "Now, let's say, for example, you worked here. Had your own division, could pick your own team. Why then I'd know we were on the same side. I'll know that I've been forgiven."

"Forgiven? For which trespass?"

"All of them."

"I want to be able to bring who I need into this investigation. Unless that is, of course, you're trying to hide something. That maybe you're behind this whole fucking shit show."

"Be careful, Sydney. I'm trying to help you."

"I'm not sure that I want that."

Bobby leaned back and looked at me for a moment. "Have you been to the training center yet?"

I didn't answer because I didn't know there was a training center. Nor did I care.

"It's the best in the world, Sydney. The best." When I just stared at him he continued. "Combat classes for you. Dog training for Blue." He gestured with his hand first at me, then over to Blue. "You know who teaches for us? Hmm?" I shook my head. "Merl."

"Merl?" My trainer. We'd only worked together for a couple months but he'd taught me how to fight and how to survive. Without Merl I'd be dead.

"It's interesting you don't keep better track of the people you care about, Sydney," Bobby said. I didn't answer him. "Would you like to see him?"

"It's always good to catch up with old acquaintances," I answered, smiling, tilting my head toward him.

"Acquaintances?" Bobby said, raising his eyebrows. "Is that what you call the people who save your life?"

I didn't answer, just maintained eye contact, trying to burrow past his walls and see what was really in there. He stared back, not flinching. Then his eyes crinkled into a hint of a smile before he bore back at me and I felt his gaze penetrate. I turned away quickly, jerking my eyes from his, unable to stop myself.

"How about tomorrow, 10 am?" He rose, buttoning his suit jacket without waiting for my answer. "Merl will meet you in the dojo. Now, if you'll excuse me, I've got to finish up some work." He extended his hand as if to help me from my chair. I stood on my own, Blue staying close. Robert stepped aside, waving his hand for me to pass. I caught his eyes for a moment, filling mine with defiance, filling them with every ounce of power I had. He smiled. "I love it when you look like that," he said.

EK

I laid awake in bed wondering and churning and turning thoughts around in my head until I couldn't take it anymore. I needed to know if Bobby was behind this entire thing. Because if he was then we were making a fatal mistake by letting him know anything about our investigation. I sat up in bed, startling Blue who looked at me expectantly. "Stay here boy, I want to check on something."

I hurried down the hall and paused outside Mulberry's room. Then I knocked quickly, rap, rap. He opened the door without a shirt on. I recognized the zig zag scar across his abdomen, the slash that puckered on his bicep, the dark hair that covered his defined pecs and abdomen. I didn't speak for a long moment as I remembered his strong arms around me, his rough kisses, the scratch of his stubble against my skin. When I finally got my eyes to his face, Mulberry was grinning. "Shut up," I said.

Mulberry laughed. "Hey, I didn't say anything. You're the one ogling me."

I pushed past him. "I wasn't ogling. I was admiring."

Mulberry closed the door behind us and followed me into the suite. "Admiring?" he said. "I like that. Mind my returning the favor? I'll gladly *admire* you."

I held up my phone. "Do you recognize this man?"

Mulberry took it and concentrated on the screen. "I don't think so."

"His name is Professor Nablestone. Is there a way you can find out if he's ever visited FGI?"

Mulberry shrugged, looking down at the photo. "I could check the logs tomorrow."

"What about tonight?"

He looked up at me. "Sydney, it's almost 3 am." I looked around the room, it was set up the same as my suite with seating around a flat screen TV. There was a beer on the coffee table and an open folder with papers spilling across the couch.

"Right," I said, shaking my head. He took a step closer and wrapped an arm around my waist. I felt the warmth of it surround me. Mulberry lowered his face to mine and smiled close. I looked up at him, our noses touching. He nuzzled me and I laughed; then he kissed me quickly. A peck, nothing more, but he held me even tighter. I placed my hands against his bare chest and looked down at them feeling his breath against my forehead. Then I closed my eyes, stood up on my toes, and closed the small space between our lips.

Mulberry's arm tensed around me, his free hand grabbing my hip and pulling me closer. He bore into me, my back bending against his arm, my hands entwined in his hair. But then he pulled his lips from mine.

"Sydney, there is something I have to tell you," he said, his arms still holding me tight, so tight I couldn't quite catch my breath.

"Mulberry," I said, it came out as a plea more than the protest I wanted to express.

"Just listen," he said, shaking me a little.

"I don't want to hear it," I said.

"You don't know what I'm going to say."

"I can't hear it. Whatever it is," I said, my heart pounding in my chest.

Mulberry frowned and released me, stepping away toward the couch. The room seemed suddenly cold. I turned and left, my bare feet silent as I traveled down the hall to my own room.

EK

Ashley was waiting in the lobby of FGI the next morning. She held two cups of ice coffee and was wearing a fitted gray jacket over a bright, flower-patterned blouse and a knee length skirt that matched the jacket. Her heels were the same pink as the blossoms on her shirt. She smiled when I came in and walked over, offering me one of the beverages.

"Thanks," I said, taking it from her. I kept walking and she fell in line opposite Blue, slightly behind and to the side of me.

"Mr. Maxim asked me to show you up to the dojo." She sounded proud to have been trusted with the task. "He thought you might enjoy a tour on the way."

"A tour?" I asked, swiping my ID and passing through the turnstile. Blue slipped under the gate and she pulled her card from her pocket and followed.

"Yes," Ashley said, catching up to me at the elevators. "To get you better acquainted with our amenities."

"Is that why you work here?" I asked her.

She smiled nervously. "This is the best organization of its kind in the world. I'm honored to work here."

"All right," I said. "Why don't you just give me the rundown on our way to the dojo."

"It would be easier to show you," she said, smiling tightly.

I shook my head. "It's already almost ten. I'm meeting someone."

"After?" she asked.

The elevator opened and we walked in. "Give me the rundown now and then, if I'm interested I'll let you show me around later." Other people got on. Buttons were pressed. "Dojo, please," I said. Someone pushed the button.

Ashley frowned. The doors closed.

"Time for the elevator pitch," I said to Ashley. There were five other people on the lift with us. All of them shared Ashley's style. I was the only one in leggings, T-shirt, and sneakers. The doors opened on the second floor and a man got off, nodding and smiling on his way out. We all nodded and smiled back. Someone mumbled "good morning."

"Start with what was on that floor," I said to Ashley as our journey began again.

"That's offices," she answered. I sipped from the coffee and nodded for her to continue. "You've seen our video rooms." I nodded again. "We also have forensic labs." The doors opened again and the man who'd pushed the button for me smiled my way.

"Your floor, I think," he said.

I laughed. "Thanks," I said, before exiting, Ashley and Blue by my sides. We were in a long corridor with laminate flooring and white walls. I could hear the squeak and bounce of a basketball game being played nearby. The smell of chlorine hung in the air. "Which way?" I asked.

Ashley lead me down the hall, away from the sports sounds and turned into another corridor. "On this level we have an amazing gym. The dojo, obviously. Racket courts," she ticked off a finger as we walked by closed doors, the sound of hard rubber balls smacking into walls emanating from inside. "Squash, basketball, a swimming pool," she kept ticking them off, like this was some type of memory quiz I was putting her through. "Climbing wall, a gun range in the basement. That's near the forensic lab."

She pushed through a door and we were in a large room lined with cardio equipment. Rows of gray machines, with TVs set into them, sat in front of a large glass window. There was a smattering of people using them. The whine of the machines and the thump of the runners feet made for a quiet soundtrack compared to the vivid scenes on the television screens. "This doesn't look like a dojo," I said.

"I know, but—," Ashly faltered. "You like to run right?"

I looked at her through narrowed eyes. "Not at a TV," I said. "Where is the dojo?"

"I'll show you."

"Now," I said, turning and walking out the door.

She continued down the hall. "We've got a great recovery unit," Ashley said, her voice nervous. "Our physical therapists are known to be the best. We have both in-patient and out-patient care. An OR even, if necessary," she said.

"For when employees get hurt?" I asked.

"Not just employees." Ashley stopped in front of another door and turned to me, a hint of pride playing across her lips, shoulders back, recovered from the cardio room encounter. "Our facility is very secure, we can keep our clients safe in their most fragile states."

"Is this the dojo?" I asked, pointing to the door.

"Yes."

"Thanks for the tour," I said, reaching for the handle.

"Do you want to learn more later?"

"Maybe tomorrow," I said.

"But—" she started, as I turned the knob.

"Fuck off, Ashley," I said. Her face reddened. "Don't take it personally, just fuck off," I said, before pushing into the dojo.

EK

The dojo had one mirrored wall, blonde hardwood floors, and picture windows that looked out into the building across the street. Merl was on the ground, facing the mirror, his legs in a wide V, his head resting on the floor between them. He was not alone. Three Doberman Pinschers stood up when I walked in. I recognized Lucy, the bitch Merl told me was the smartest dog he'd ever know. Michael, a large and intimidating beast, stood closest to him on the right. Next to Michael was a dog with ears still soft and floppy with puppyhood. "Sydney," Merl said, looking up at me with a warm smile.

I felt tears prick at my eyes. He was the first person to ever know me as Sydney Rye and hearing my name in his voice called me back to our time on a Mexican beach, when he'd challenged me to live. "Merl, it's so good to see you." Blue stayed by my side but I could feel his enthusiasm. He was excited to see Merl and his other friends, too.

I crossed the room and Merl stood up to meet me in a hug. He still wore all black, cargo pants tucked into army boots, tight black T-shirt, long ponytail that held his black ringlets away from his face. "Ready to train?" he asked.

"Merl," I said, stepping away from him. "You really work for FGI now?"

He shrugged. "On a contract basis. I come in every couple months. Teach seminars regularly."

"Oh."

"Why?"

"No, it's just Bobby Maxim made it seem like you worked here, full time."

"Office politics, that's not a game I've ever been adept at."

"Will you teach me throwing stars?" I blurted out.

He laughed. "Let's start with some Tai Chi practice."

I looked over at the youngest of his dogs, who was staring at Blue like he would give just about anything to try tackling him. "Who's this guy?" I asked.

Merl turned to the young pup whose tail began to thump rhythmically under his master's gaze. "One of Thunder's puppies."

"Where's Thunder?" I asked and then instantly knew. "Oh, Merl, I'm sorry."

Merl turned back to me and smiled. "It's okay, everything dies."

"Always so uplifting to see you," I said with a smile.

"Ah, are we still hiding from that truth Sydney?"

"Let's just do some Tai Chi," I offered.

Merl laughed and agreed. We practiced for forty five minutes, Merl leading, then watching. "Relax your fingers. Not that much. Yes, like that. We are fighting a battle, Sydney not serving cocktails. Good. Keep your weight more even, yes, never lose touch with the ground. Excellent," and so on.

When I felt as though I was floating on my feet, completely free of any thoughts but the deep understanding of how my body moved, there was a knock at the door. All four dogs turned their heads toward the sound. Lucy and Blue both rose to their feet as Bobby Maxim walked in. He smiled at us. "I hope I'm not interrupting but I wanted to take Sydney over to the shooting range before my next meeting. You don't mind do you, Merl?"

"Of course not," Merl answered. "Sydney, would you like to have lunch after?"

"Yes," I said with a smile.

We had the shooting gallery to ourselves. We'd checked out weapons from an employee behind a cage, but now we were alone in the big empty room full of bullet holes. There were seven lanes. Ours was in the center of the room.

"I know Merl doesn't believe in guns, but you do," Bobby said as he filled a clip with bullets.

"I use what comes my way," I answered, eyeing the AR-15 rifle we'd brought in with us. It was resting on a table that ran along the back wall behind the lanes. A convenient place to keep your extra guns and ammunition.

"Go ahead," Robert said, catching my gaze.

I picked it up, light but substantial. Pulling out the magazine, I began filling it, using a speed loader. The bullets were tapered at the end, the casings looked like cheap gold. The kind of gold my mother might have worn during her drinking days. The magazine full and in place, I adjusted the handle length. The gun was light, it felt good and easy in my hands. When I looked through the scope, a small red dot marked where my bullet would go.

"This range is a little short for that gun," Bobby admitted. "Most of our rifle training is done out of town at our outdoor range."

I lowered the gun and Bobby handed me earmuffs and protective eyewear, then loaded a target onto the mount and sent it backward, the bottom of the flimsy paper fluttering up as the pulley system took it down the room. It was orange with a white silhouette of a man's top half on it, the bullseye in his stomach. "How'd you learn to shoot, Sydney?" Bobby asked me as the paper came to a halt.

"I grew up around hunting," I paused. "And drug dealing."

Bobby smiled.

"What about you?" I asked.

He brought his protection over his ears. "Similar."

I pulled on my earmuffs and turned toward the target. Raising the AR-15 I placed the red dot in the center of the target. "Seems almost like cheating," I said.

"What does?" Bobby asked.

"The red dot," I answered before pulling the trigger. It projected the bullet straight into the bullseye of my target with hardly a kickback. I smiled and pulled the trigger again, enlarging the hole I'd already made. I lowered the gun and turned to Bobby. "You want a turn?" I asked, holding out the rifle, muzzle to the ceiling, safety on.

He laughed. "Sydney Rye, do you think I'd really turn my back on you around a loaded weapon?"

I pointed to the gun in his hand. "What about that?"

"You know I don't want to kill you, and if I did want to kill you, I wouldn't do it in here. But you, Ms. Rye, are crazy," he grinned.

"I resent that," I said with a smile. "I wouldn't shoot you in the back."

Bobby laughed. "I feel so much better. Now, why don't you keep practicing and I'll watch."

"What's the point?"

"I want to see how good you are."

"You show me yours and I'll show you mine," I said with a smile, "isn't that how it works?"

Bobby smiled but didn't answer.

"Come on, show me what you got."

Bobby laughed and then pushed past me to face the target. I stepped back. He took aim with the handgun. I looked the length of the room to where my target sat with its two bullseyes. A shot rang out, the casing launched into the air and bounced off the wall, landing at my feet with a small metallic ting. Looking at the target I saw a bullet hole in the center of the shadow man's forehead.

"Lucky shot," I said.

Bobby squeezed the trigger all 17 times creating a smiling face and buttons down his chest. He put the empty gun down and reached up, flicking the switch to bring the target back to us. A smile played across his lips and his eyes lightened.

"Ex Navy Seal?" I asked.

He laughed. The target returned to us with a clunk. Bobby turned to it and took it off its clips, replacing it with another. I held the rifle in my hands, still loaded. He was right in front of me, his back turned as he clipped the new target into place. I could click off the safety. He turned around so fast I startled at his quick movement. Before I knew what was happening the gun was taken from me. "I can hear you thinking," he said, his face close to mine, the gun securely in his hands.

He stepped back. "Try the handgun," he offered. "You can reload, I'll keep this for you." He smiled and I walked past him to the handgun, exhaling a deep breath as I went. I reloaded the magazine, feeling the slippery surface of each shell, admiring their rounded tips. I've always thought there was something beautiful about bullets, ever since I was a kid.

The gun reloaded, I sent the target down the line, about as far as it had been. I turned to look at Bobby who leaned against the wall, the rifle resting by his hand. I couldn't see if the safety was on or off. Had I clicked it off? Was that the sound he heard? That I didn't even know I'd made? But how could he hear that with hearing protection on?

Returning my attention to the target, I raised the gun. It was light and my hands were steady as I lined up the white dots, three in a row, and fired. The gun stayed steady, hardly a jump at all. I thought about the guns I'd used in India, they kicked like horses, my wrists, shoulders, and fingers sore for days. That wouldn't happen with this bad boy. And my aim wasn't bad either. I squinted down the line and saw that I was almost dead center, bullseye. I raised the gun and tapped the silhouette of a man between the eyes. Then I gave him two eyes. The one to the left was not as high as the one to the right. My man's smile was crooked and the buttons down his chest not entirely even but I thought it was pretty good.

"We could teach you to make that a straight line," Bobby said as I brought in the target.

"Don't know if that's something I need to know," I answered, pulling off my ear protection. "Not often I'm shooting a still target that far off with a handgun."

A man came in wearing a dark suit and bright blue tie, he was young and eager looking. "Sir," he said to Bobby. Maxim pulled his earmuffs off and the man continued. "You asked me to remind you."

Bobby looked down at his watch. "Right, I'll be right there." He handed the man his rifle. "Take care of this for me." The man took it like he'd held the weapon before.

"Yes, sir," he said, then turned and left.

"Don't tell me he's not ex-something military," I said.

Bobby smiled. "I can offer you the best training in the world, the best equipment and technology. What is it that you want?"

I turned away from him and unclipped my target. I could feel his annoyance. Bobby Maxim was not used to people turning their back on him. Rolling up the target I turned, shaking my head. "You can't give me what I want."

His lips pursed and a light flush of color rose on his cheeks. "Tell me," he said, his voice low and threatening.

I leaned back against the barrier between me and the shooting lanes. "I want Hugh exonerated from all charges."

"That takes time."

I narrowed my eyes. "But you have a plan for how to do it?"

A smile touched his lips, and I knew I'd blown it. He'd heard the hope in my voice. The obvious truth that I did not have a plan and was looking for a good one.

"Yes, Sydney," Maxim said. "I always have a plan."

Holding up the hand gun I asked, "If I promise not to shoot you with this, can I keep it?"

Bobby laughed. "Sure," he said, pushing off against the wall and turning toward the exit. "See you later," he said over his shoulder before passing through the doors. They swung back and forth for a moment until resting in place.

I looked around the big empty room and decided I wanted to shoot some more.

CHAPTER FIFTEEN
TRUTHS AND CHOICES

The restaurant Merl took me to was tucked into a back street of downtown Miami. It was late for the regular lunch crowd and we had the place mostly to ourselves. The restaurant's garden area was nestled between taller buildings so that shade covered the yard. The menu was vegetarian, the waiter wore dreadlocks, and the scent of strong marijuana hung in the air.

Our waiter wasn't delighted by the presence of *four* dogs, but he brought them bowls of waters and then ignored them. Merl ordered us both green juice specials and falafel platters, assuring me that I would love the energy it gave me. I nodded with a sarcastic look on my face.

Settling back against the rattan chair I laid my menu on the metal table. "So, how have you been?" Merl asked.

"It's been a long time. Almost four years."

"Yes, a lot has changed."

"For us both, I imagine. When did you lose Thunder?" I asked.

"About four months ago," he answered, blinking his long lashes.

"I'm so sorry," I said, leaning forward and laying one of my hands over his.

"Thanks," he said, looking down at the dogs resting at our feet.

Turning back to me he asked, "How are you doing with your loss? Is it any better?"

I shrugged and smiled. "I think it is." I paused and took a deep breath. "Something happened."

"Yes?"

I looked up into his deep, warm eyes. "I hired mourners," I said.

"Mourners?"

"Yes, professional mourners, in Udaipur, India. Women wearing long black dresses who cried and wailed for my loss. And it let me...I don't know. It let something loose in me." I closed my eyes remembering that night when I'd stood on my balcony overlooking the city, its lake sparkling in the moonlight while the mourners below undulated and screamed. I could feel the grief course through me and out of me. Then Mulberry had found me, wailing on my balcony, and we'd...I opened my eyes, trying to figure out how to explain the shift, so subtle yet clearly different.

"It's not that the hole is gone," Merl said. "Maybe just that now you feel as though you may be able to fill it again?"

"I think that might be right," I answered.

The waiter returned with tall glasses filled with chlorophyll green drinks and we both leaned back so that he could place them in front of us. The drink smelled of freshly cut grass. A smell I love, just not in my beverages.

"I'm glad to hear that," Merl said as the waiter left us. "That you're feeling different. I, too, have gone through some," he smiled and shrugged, "changes of heart, perhaps, is what we should call it."

"Oh really?" I said, smiling.

The waiter returned again, this time with our food. Merl watched him leave, the restaurant door closing him inside where the air conditioning hummed. Merl turned to me. "I know Dan told you about Joyful Justice."

I straightened, the hairs on my arms raising. Blue sat up and looked at me, his gaze keen. Merl put his hand on my forearm. "Sydney, calm down, you're hyperventilating."

I realized he was right and sat back, taking several deep breaths.

Leaning forward I took a sip of the green drink; it tasted like sweet grass with bitter edges, but it felt good going down.

"You don't want Joyful Justice to exist?"

"No, I don't want it to exist," I snapped. "Of course not. It's ridiculous. All those people on that site are following a fictional character. I was never that person. I did not avenge my brother's death. That would be Bobby Maxim. They should go fucking worship at his feet."

"Eat something," Merl said, pointing to my plate. "You'll feel better."

I didn't argue, instead inhaling the delicious falafels after wrapping them in a pita and dousing them in yogurt and hot sauces. Then I dipped my fries into the leftover sauces before finally licking my fingers and sitting back. Merl was quiet as well, his energy calm and collected, like always. My belly felt very full and I suddenly wanted a nap. The waiter came back out and took our coffee order, removing the empty plates.

"Now Sydney, I understand that you are not ready to hear about Joyful Justice, but we've reached a point where we have no choice."

"Who is we?" I asked. Blue shifted, resting his head into my lap and I laid my hand onto his head. "You're a member of Joyful Justice?"

Merl pursed his lips and gave a curt nod, but before I could ask another question he cut me off. "First, I need you to know that I can't give you much information at this time. But not telling you started to feel more like a lie than a safety precaution."

"Safety precaution?" I asked. "What the hell does that mean? And since when are you a vigilante?" I said, keeping my voice a whisper so that it wouldn't turn into a scream.

"You obviously realize how much bigger Joyful Justice is than you. As you said, it's based on a fictional character, an idea, a martyr in fact."

"A martyr? Merl—"

He waved me silent before I could continue. Taking my free hand in his he squeezed it softly. "You changed my life, you changed the way that I saw the world and what I wanted out of it. And I'm not the only one."

"You're the one who told me I was a freakin' idiot—"

He cut me off again. "What you did was idiotic. I don't believe that violence is the only solution or that you should run off half-cocked not caring if you live or die. But what you taught me is that the strong must protect the weak. And the best way to gain strength, Sydney, is through connections. Through a network of people who protect and support you."

"Is Mulberry a member?" I asked.

He nodded. "It was decided that I should be the one to tell you."

"But Dan—"

"He wasn't supposed to do that."

"So you all agreed on how to deal with me?" I asked, licking my lips, feeling light-headed.

"Yes, and now you have a choice on how to treat all of us. You can join us Sydney, become a member, choose to be a part of something bigger than yourself, bigger than any person can be on their own. Or you can be pissed about how you inspired us all."

He let my hand go and stood, his dogs rising to their feet. The waiter came out carrying a single cup of coffee. "I'll see you soon," Merl said as he dropped some money on the table. Then he turned and left, his dogs following close behind.

EK

I paid and was sipping my coffee when Mulberry called. "I checked the logs. Doesn't look like Professor Nablestone has ever visited the office."

"Okay," I said.

He continued, his voice more upbeat. "Some good news, it looks like Santiago was right," he said. "Hugh came back positive for datura."

"Great," I said.

"Everything all right?" he asked.

"Where are you?"

"I'm at the office."

"Meet me where we jog," I said. "We need to talk."

I hung up and when he called back I didn't answer. Driving over the causeway toward Miami Beach I wondered what to do. I trusted Mulberry cared about me and that in his mind everything he did was for my own good. But I also knew that sometimes when he tried to protect me he made mistakes. I needed to know what was going on.

I parked near our spot, then Blue and I walked the short block to the shaded space under our tree. I sat down on the wall and Blue sat on the sidewalk next to me. It was hot even in the shade. Blue panted. I felt sweat gather at my hairline and between my breasts.

Mulberry showed up holding his suit jacket, his sleeves rolled up and sweat dappling his dress shirt. "What's going on?" he asked, standing over me.

"You tell me, Mulberry. One minute you admit to know about Joyful Justice, and the next I find out that you're a member of it."

He licked his lips. "I tried to tell you."

"When?"

"Last night," he said, an edge of anger in his voice.

"Yeah, well, that still woulda been a little late."

He sat down on the wall next to me, not so that we were touching but I felt the heat coming off him anyway. "Sydney, you made it pretty clear to Dan, Malina, and anyone else who was paying attention that bringing up Joyful Justice made you mad. See, see," he said pointing at my face. "You should see your expression right now."

"How can you possibly think this is a good idea?" I asked, trying to keep the anger I felt out of my voice.

It didn't work. Mulberry puffed himself up, just like Blue and his hackles, I thought. "You try and pretend like you don't need anyone, Sydney, but that's bullshit. I'm not afraid to admit that I need people in my life. People who care about the same things as me. People who are striving for something bigger in this world."

"Since when are you striving for the same things as me," I whispered so that I wouldn't yell it. "You work for goddamn Robert Maxim."

He didn't answer but turned away from me. "Wait," I said. "Hold on," I stood up. "Is he involved with Joyful Justice?"

Mulberry almost laughed as he looked up at me. "No," he said, sounding fully amused.

"Then how can you work for him and for Joyful Justice"?

"We can't talk about that."

"Because I'm not a member of Joyful Justice! Are you kidding me?"

"Keep your voice down."

I gripped my hands into fists, feeling my nails dig into my palm, rage pouring through me. "Keep my voice down?" I hissed. "All my friends are in some secret society, named after me I might add. And you are all keeping secrets from me. Secrets that gravely affect my life." I flattened my palm on my chest, feeling indignation mix with anger and hurt bring tears to my eyes.

"It's named after Joy Humbolt. Last time I checked your passport reads Sydney Rye." He smiled at me and patted the top of the wall next to him. "Sydney, we want you to join us. That's what everyone wants."

I did not take his invitation to sit down. "The only way you'll tell me what is going on is if I join the team?"

"Yes."

"This is some kind of sick joke. You won't tell me why you work at FGI, you won't tell me why Hugh is facing murder charges."

Mulberry held up a hand. "I don't know why that's happening. I don't think Robert set Hugh up."

"Why not?"

"He's been watching this Joyful Justice thing as closely as anyone. Robert thought you living with Dan away from it all was great. He didn't want you back in action. He had a pretty good guess which side you'd fall on. But he knew that the Hugh thing would bring you back so now he's trying to seduce you into accepting his kind of power instead of asserting your own. He doesn't want to face you. And that's why I encouraged you to act like you were considering the idea of working for him. It was safest for you not to know. That way he figured it wasn't happening. Robert Maxim doesn't see the true power of your mythology."

"You don't think I can keep a secret?"

He caught my eyes. "You didn't want to hear it, Sydney. Admit that at least."

"Didn't want to hear what you all were up to, why not?"

"Because you might have been able to stop it. And now you can't."

I bit my lip, squeezing the flesh hard between my teeth. "Would I have to follow orders?" I asked.

Mulberry laughed and grinned. "None of us are dumb enough to think that you're going to follow orders."

"Do I get to give them?"

"It's more collaborative than that."

"Can we kill Bobby Maxim?"

"Maybe."

I sat down next to him and we rested in silence, feeling the humid heat around us, sweat trickling down our bodies. I looked over at him. "I don't think I can do it," I said.

"Maybe not yet," he answered.

My phone rang, and I fished it out of my bag. It was Dan.

"Hey," Dan said. He sounded excited. "Come over?"

"Over where?" I asked, watching two guys skateboard toward us, sharing an easy conversation. One of them laughed as they passed.

"My house, it's only about a two-hour drive and I've got a lot of stuff to show you."

"What kind of stuff at your house?"

Mulberry looked over at me, a question mark on his brow.

"You'll see, just come over. I'll text you the directions. Get here as soon as you can."

We hung up and the text came through. "Looks like I'm headed down to the Keys," I said.

"To see Dan?" Mulberry asked.

"Yes."

Mulberry stood up, holding his jacket. "When will you be back?"

Looking up at the waning sun I answered, "By the time I get down there and hear what he has to say, I might just stay the night rather than drive home at that hour." Mulberry didn't say anything, but his grip tightened on his jacket, twisting the fabric. "That's not a problem, is it?" I asked.

"No, not a problem. I look forward to hearing his findings."

"Maybe you should come."

"Can't," he shook his head. "I've got cases besides Hugh's I'm working on."

"What's up with you and Dan?" I asked, a lump of anxiety raising in my throat. "I mean, you guys are working on Joyful Justice together and..." I let the "and" hang in the air because I didn't have the words for what was going on with me and them.

Mulberry shook his head, a small, rueful smile on his lips, eyes cast to the ground. "I don't know," he said, shrugging. "He had a right to be pissed at me, then he told you about Joyful Justice so I had a right to be pissed at him, but really," he looked up at me, "I respect the hell out of him and if *you* weren't his girl..." He ran a hand through his hair and it stayed on its end.

"I'm not his girl," I said.

"Well, that's just it, isn't' it?" Mulberry said, his words coming quickly. "You're not either of ours, so really there is nothing to fight about."

"Right," I smiled. "But you still want to punch him in the face."

"So bad," Mulberry admitted with a small smile. "But I still like him. I still think he's amazing at what he does and Joyful Justice couldn't happen without him."

"So, you're fine working together."

He nodded but I could see a secret lurking behind his eyes. "What?" I asked. "What is going on?"

He shook his head. "Nothing."

"Liar," I said, angry again. I stood up and began to walk away but Mulberry grabbed my arm with his free hand.

"We just both agreed," he bit his lip. "We agreed to stay away from you in that way. You know," he smiled again, and there was something in his eyes that I'd never seen before, some kind of rock he was standing on. "For the good of the cause."

"Ugh," was all I could say.

CHAPTER SIXTEEN
DINNER AND DATURA

Dan lived in a bungalow on Marathon Island in the Keys. His place was single story and painted white. The curtains were drawn and the grass that covered the small yard was yellow. The house was dwarfed by its more prosperous neighbors, which were raised on stilts above bright green lawns. I pulled into the driveway and parked in front of the garage door.

Climbing out I stretched my arms toward the sky and then bent down and wrapped my fingers around my ankles feeling the muscles around my spine and down the back of my legs release slowly. Blue jumped out of the car and sniffed the dying grass along the side of the driveway. When I finished stretching, I rang the front doorbell.

"It's unlocked," Dan call from inside.

I walked into a living room that was painted a cheerful yellow with white wood panelling up to shoulder height. A slouchy couch and matching armchairs faced a coffee table and flat screen TV. "In here," Dan called. I followed his voice through the living room and into a kitchen with big windows looking out onto a canal. The back door was open and I walked out to find Dan over a grill. "Hey," he said with a smile. "Who's hungry?"

We ate giant shrimps marinated in Teriyaki sauce with grilled pineapple, onion, and peppers over white rice. He even had a steak for Blue. "You're spoiling him," I commented.

"Come on, he deserves it," Dan answered. Blue finished up his steak and came to Dan's side, leaning into him and staring up into his face as though Dan were the king of the world and deserved all good things.

"I guess," I said, watching them.

"Another beer?" Dan asked.

"Sure," I stood up with him to help clear the plates. "I can do the dishes," I offered.

"Really?" he said, looking over at me, an eyebrow raised.

"You cooked," I said.

He laughed. "Sydney Rye acting domestic. I never thought I'd see the day." Blue followed Dan back into the kitchen and sat attentively as he scraped his plate and put it into the dishwasher. I washed the few dishes that remained while Dan wiped down the counters and hummed a song I didn't recognize. The kitchen and table cleaned up, Dan led me into his office. Three large screens took up one wall and a half-moon shaped desk faced them. On the desk was a keyboard and a half-drunk glass of water. Dan grabbed a stool from by the door and placed it next to the swivel chair facing the center of the desk.

"Sit," he said. I hopped onto the stool and Dan sat in the chair. "Okay," he leaned forward and tapped on the keyboard which brought all three screens to life. Using his mouse Dan guided an arrow to the first screen where a window displayed green numbers changing against a black background.

"Here I've been tracking cases where people woke up from committing crimes, anything from robbery to rape to murder, without any memory of the act. Also, people who were victims of crimes who have no memories of the event. Now, obviously, we can't assume that every case where a person woke up without memory of their crime involved datura. It's basically never tested for in this country. But I think it's a good source of data to have."

I watched as his fingers glided over the keyboard and windows on the screens changed. "I've also been looking deeper into Professor Nablestone. I read those papers he mentioned to us and found some really interesting stuff."

Several articles popped up into the center screen. "Now, I've told you about the way they use the drug in Colombia to rob people and that most of the victims have no memory of the incident." I felt a shiver run down my spine and goosebumps spread across my flesh. It was horrible and it was brilliant. Couldn't this same drug that wiped your memory clean when used for evil do the same when used for good?

"Hey," I realized Dan was looking at me. "You okay?"

I nodded. "Yeah, go on."

Dan nodded. "But here is the thing. The drug doesn't always wipe out any memory. If you just ate the seeds right off the plant or brewed them into tea you wouldn't be as pliable and you'd have, from all accounts, horrific, realistic hallucinations."

"I guess that actually sounds worse."

"From what I've gathered about Professor Nablestone's research he is developing all sorts of datura-based drugs. They can make you pliable, give you intense hallucinations, and some of them can cause permanent brain damage."

"And it's just a white powder that can be blown in your face?"

"That's right."

"God, that's scary."

"In Colombia, prostitutes put cotton up their noses and then wipe it on their lips so that when they kiss their johns they just 'fall away'."

"I can see why you'd want to weaponize it," I said.

"Yeah. So here's the question. Who would pay for this research to be done?" Dan turned back to his keyboard.

"Didn't Lawrence Taggert's wife's money come from her family's pharmaceutical company?" I asked, my brain rotating the facts, trying them all at different angles.

"I was just getting to that," Dan said, looking up at me with a smile. He tapped on the keys some more and a photograph appeared on the right screen of Professor Nablestone with his arm around Lawrence

Taggert's wife. They looked like they were at some kind of gala. Her hair was up and she wore a silk shift dress. Professor Nablestone had on a nice suit, gray and green with a white shirt and paisley tie that brought out the green in his eyes. Behind them, well-dressed people mingled, holding wine glasses.

"And look at this." He zoomed in on the photograph, centering on a group of people behind them. "Recognize that guy?" Dan asked as the picture refocused.

"Holy shit," I said. "That's Robert Maxim."

"The one and the same."

"Where is this?"

"It was taken about six years ago at a fundraiser for Professor Nablestone's research center in the Everglades."

"The one in the pamphlet?"

"Right. And Mrs. Taggert's pharmaceutical company is by far the biggest donor to Professor Nablestone's research."

I leaned back on my stool.

Dan turned to me. "So," he said. "What we've got are some connections but no motive. Why would Professor Nablestone or Taggert's wife, or anyone with access to the datura, kill Lawrence and set up Hugh to take the fall?"

"Lightning," I said.

"Meaning?"

I sat forward and looked at the image of Robert Maxim on the screen, he was smiling at an attractive woman, holding a glass of red wine loosely in his hand. "Hugh was saying that he thinks violence might be like lightning. If it strikes you once, you're more likely to get hit again."

"All right," Dan said. "So let's say we take Hugh out of the equation. Say he was just an innocent bystander, not actually the one under attack."

"Your search," I said, glancing at the green numbers dancing across the black background. "You're looking for victims, too?"

"Yes."

"Did you check out how many were last seen at one of Ivan's clubs?"

"Of course," he said with a smile. "Five so far, and that's only the ones who admitted it, remember."

"You have a theory?" I asked.

"What if Ivan was somehow getting ahold of some of Professor Nablestone's stuff?"

"You don't think Nablestone would have sold it to him?"

Dan shook his head. "Guy is fastidious. He wouldn't expose himself like that."

"Fastidious?"

Dan sat forward and smiled. "I've searched through a lot of computers," he said. "And I've never seen one like this. Deep deep encryption. Took me a long time to get in. And then what do I find?"

I leaned forward, excited. "What?"

"Nothing. Perfectly organized nothing."

"Nothing?"

"His internet activity, not only cleared, but when recovered, totally boring. He reads professional sites, streams a little opera, and looks at occasional vanilla porn."

"Okay?"

"That's just weird. Here's a guy seemingly obsessed with his research, yet virtually nothing of that nature is on his computer. Plus, he appears to have almost no social life and his car spends all its time either at the university or in the Everglades. Maybe he keeps everything interesting on paper," Dan laughed. "But more likely he's got a computer that is never online. And that would mean there is a very small group of people involved. They can't be on a network or I'd find them. So if he's that careful just with the notes about what he's making, do you think he'd sell the actual product to a thug like Ivan?"

"So you think someone was stealing it?"

"And selling it to Ivan." Dan said.

"Ivan said that Lawrence provided what no one else had. Do you think he was talking about Datura? Was Lawrence providing it?"

"It's possible," Dan said.

"So who killed him? Who is the puppet master?"

Dan's fingers returned to the keyboard and windows began to pop onto the left hand screen. "I think it was Nablestone, himself."

"Really?" I thought about the footage from the front of the restaurant. The man behind the umbrella, the expert at staying hidden. The man who didn't flinch. It could be Nablestone. The way he'd adjusted his cap, moved his body, it was certainly fastidious, I thought. But that was just grasping at straws.

"I don't think he'd trust anyone else with it. And, I think this guy is a real sicko."

"Because of the computer?"

"The vanilla porn." His fingers kept typing.

"Excuse me?"

"He just went to those sites in order to create the veneer of normality, his computer was complete fiction. I don't think he gets off on sex. I think it's power." Dan pointed to the screens. "I think he did it before." When he saw my expression he hurried to add, "Not killing someone. But look." I flicked my eyes to the screen. A news story with the caption "President of University Streaks Football Game." The picture showed a naked man, his intimates pixelated for decency, overweight and grimacing with effort as he ran across a field. Several football players were in the shot, stock still, all eyes on the nude figure. "Dr. Nablestone's former boss," Dan said. "Has no memory of the incident. Came to within minutes of being tackled to the ground by security."

"That's circumstantial," I said. "But kind of compelling."

"I bet I find more."

His fingers returned to the keys. "All reports," Dan said, "of men waking up with their last memory at one of Ivan's clubs," he said as files opened on the screen.

I nodded my head, pressing my lips together. "Were any of them tested for datura?"

"They were tested for Rohypnol but nothing came up. I sent these over to Mulberry to see if there were any samples left to test. If we could match what was in Hugh to them, then we've got more evidence."

"Do you know if Nablestone has an alibi?"

"According to his calendar he was at the opera," Dan answered. "He has a subscription."

"What do you think his TAs know?"

"I think the girl knows more than the guy."

"Maybe they're sleeping together."

Dan laughed. "I don't think that girl has gotten laid in a while."

I grimaced. "Come on," I said. "Every girl who's a bitch just needs to get laid?"

Dan threw up his hands. "Whoa, I was just joking around." Then cracking a smile, "You are acting kind of bitchy right now though...so."

"Shut up," I swatted at him. He swiveled his chair away laughing and apologized. Dan laid his hands back on the keys and began to type. "What about Ivan?" I asked.

"What do you mean?"

"Let's say he didn't kill Lawrence. What's going to happen to him?"

"What do you mean?" Dan asked, turning to me.

"One of the girls who worked there, she had ligature marks on her wrists and ankles," I said, looking over at him. When he'd gotten on that plane with Anita, she'd had those marks on her limbs. They told of much more horror than a thin bruise.

"I know," he answered.

"Mulberry told you?"

Dan bit his lip. "Was I not supposed to tell you that?" he asked.

"I don't know, Dan. I'm not sure what I'm not supposed to know," I said, feeling anger bubble up.

"Okay," Dan put his hands up in the air. "Don't get mad at me. If you want to scream at someone, call Mulberry or Malina. I wanted to tell you everything from the beginning."

"What is everything?"

A pained expression passed over his face. "I can't tell you."

"What?" I said, low and dangerous.

"Seriously, Sydney. I can't tell you Joyful Justice business."

"This is too ridiculous," I said, throwing up my hands. "I'm leaving."

I stood up and Dan did, too. He reached out and held my bicep. "Hey, Sydney. Stop."

I turned around and looked up into his grape-green eyes. They were pale in the computer's glow. He blinked at me. "Dan," I said, my voice softer than before. "I can't just join Joyful Justice and ride off into the sunset with you all. I think it's crazy what you're doing. And dangerous."

"Since when are you afraid of danger?"

"I'm not," I said. "Not for me. But I couldn't stand it. In fact, I can't stand it that you are all risking...well, you're risking everything for...I don't even know what."

"For justice, Joy."

Dan had never called me Joy before. The name passed through his lips, soft and almost aching.

"That's crazy," I said.

"Then I guess we're all nuts. You included."

I pursed my lips. "I'm not crazy," I said.

"Sure you are. Now come on and sit down. We have more to go over. You can leave in the morning in a huff if you want, but for now let's try and do what we can to help Hugh, okay?"

"Fine," I said, climbing back up onto the stool. "What else do you have?"

Dan and I went over cases of memory loss for another two hours until my eyelids got heavy and my head began to nod forward. "Come on," Dan said. "Time for bed."

EK

I followed him down the hall to his room. And when I saw the queen size bed in the middle of the space I paused in the doorway. "I'm going to take the couch," Dan said. "I'll probably work for a few more hours, though." I nodded. "Here's a towel and you can borrow a T-shirt." He rummaged around in his drawers until he found an old white T-shirt. I took it from his hand, feeling the worn cotton against my fingers, reminding me of him, of how we used to be. When we'd run away from life together and lived like nothing else mattered.

Well, I guess in hindsight he'd still been thinking life in the larger world mattered. Apparently he'd been setting up Joyful Justice without me even knowing. I thought again about Hugh telling me that people only see what they want to see so it's easy to hide from them. I'd used that knowledge for great effect over the years, but this was the first time I could see so clearly it applied to everyone, even those of us who knew the secret.

"The bathroom is in here," Dan said, opening a door. "I'll see you in the morning." He walked toward the exit and paused, his hand on the knob. "Sleep well." And then he left me alone in his bedroom.

I washed my face and changed into the big white T-shirt, feeling it against my skin brought a deep sadness. A longing for something I'd lost, something it was possible had only existed in my mind. A chance at normalcy. A chance to love and be loved without the burdens and dangers of being Sydney Rye.

I climbed between Dan's sheets. Blue hopped up next to me, but instead of taking his place at the foot of the bed he laid by my side, snuggling close. He sighed once and then lowered his head and breathed evenly. I threw an arm around his shoulders and buried my face in his neck. Inhaling his musky dog scent, I began to cry. Silent tears poured down my face and I felt a hiccup of a sob rise in my throat. I let it out, forcing the sound into Blue's neck, hoping that Dan would not hear, but also hoping he might. That he would come back and hold me and tell me that it was all going to be all right.

I woke up and fluttered my eyelids, seeing the room in the soft light of dawn. Blue was at my feet, having crept out of my embrace at some point while I slept. The curtains were open and I could see the sunlight straining to pass through the broad leaves of a palm tree. I rolled over and saw Dan asleep in his reading chair, his feet up on the ottoman, his head cocked to one side. He looked uncomfortable and I thought he'd wake with a stiff neck.

Climbing out of bed I crossed the room toward him. I reached out to gently shake his shoulder but stopped before touching him. Taking a moment to admire his features, the way his hair was always in his eyes, the way his chest rose and fell with each breath. "Sydney," he muttered, but didn't open his eyes.

"Dan," I said. "Come to bed. You'll hurt yourself sleeping in that chair."

A gentle smile crossed his face and he reached out for me, pulling me into his lap. He tucked my head under his chin and I heard his breathing steady and realized he was asleep. I laid in his arms for a moment, his arm wrapped around my waist, hand spread across my belly. I looked down at his forearm, let my fingers wander over the soft hair that grew there. I closed my eyes and let the raising and falling of his chest lull me back to sleep.

When I woke up again, I was back in the bed. I rolled over and Dan was gone. The chair stood empty, not giving up any secrets. I wondered if it had been a dream. Dressing quickly I brushed my teeth and ran my fingers through my hair. Dan was on the living room couch in his boxers, one arm thrown across his face, a sheet laying crumpled on the floor.

I took Blue into the yard and watched him inspect the bougainvillea that climbed one side of Dan's fence. Then he went over to the canal and bent toward it, his nostrils flaring with interest. "Coffee?" Dan said behind me, making me jump. "Sorry, didn't mean to scare you."

"No, it's fine," I said, taking the steaming cup he offered me. "I was just zoning out."

"Well, don't let me keep you from that all important activity. I'm in the office. Come in whenever you're ready."

I sat on Dan's back porch watching Blue and sipping coffee for another twenty minutes and then decided I would try my hand at breakfast. I had a sudden deep need for pancakes. I found flour, eggs and milk, a bowl and a pan. Spatula, too. Blue sat and watched me move clumsily around the kitchen. I dumped what looked like the right amount of flour into the bowl and then cracked two eggs on top. I couldn't find a whisk so used a fork to begin mixing up my concoction. Adding milk made it easier to stir but the lumps that formed in my batter appeared to be permanent. I decided I didn't mind and turned to the pan. Finding butter in the back of the fridge, I cut off a sizable chunk and left it to melt in the pan while I looked for a ladle for my batter. The first pancake went in and I watched its lumpy surface hoping I'd know when to turn it. Pancakes were the one thing my mother made on regular basis throughout my childhood, though hers never had lumps. Often she'd even make smiley faces with chocolate chips and whip cream.

With that in mind I turned away from my first pancake and began rifling through Dan's cabinets on the hunt for chocolate chips. I didn't find any but by the time I'd given up the underside of my first pancake was smoking. I flipped it over and stared at the dark brown surface wondering if I should just throw the whole thing away when I heard Blue barking. Realizing I'd left the back door open, I looked out and saw Blue posturing in front of some kind of creature. He hopped to one side and I realized it was a skunk. "Blue," I yelled. He hopped to the other side, preventing the skunk from leaving. It began to turn as if to spray him. "Blue," I called louder, "Come!" He turned his head and seeing me in the doorway took off full speed toward me, his tongue flapping out of his mouth with excitement. The skunk still sprayed and as Blue skittered into the kitchen I slammed the door. I ran around to all the windows and slammed them shut.

"What's going on?" Dan asked right as the smoke alarm began to sound.

"Shit, my pancake," I said, running to the stove and turning it off. Grabbing a hot mitt from a drawer, Dan picked up the pan and dropped it into the sink, turning on the cold water and causing steam to pour out of the smoking pan.

"Why are you closing the windows?" Dan asked. He went to open the one closest to him, to let some of the pancake smoke out, but I grabbed his arm.

"A skunk," I said.

And then the smell hit us. The scent of the skunk spray combined with burnt-pancake smoke made us both start to cough. I took Dan's hand and ran out of the kitchen, through the house, and to the front door. Pushing it open I pulled Dan down into his driveway where the air was still fresh, though I figured the skunk spray would get there eventually. "Maybe we should go out for breakfast," I suggested.

Dan looked over at me and began to laugh. Soon his hands were on his knees and tears ran down his face as he kept laughing. "What?" I asked. He waved a hand at me.

"It's just so funny," he said.

I put a hand on my hip. "What's so funny?"

"You," he said, wiping the tears off his face. "Trying to make pancakes."

"What? I can't make pancakes?"

"Apparently not," Dan said, the laughter starting all over again.

"Come on," I said, pushing him toward my car, Blue by my side. "Get in, I'm buying."

After breakfast I dropped Dan at his place and headed back toward Miami. Mulberry called as I drove over the 7 Mile Bridge, aqua water stretching all around me, the hum of my tires almost silent.

"How did it go?" Mulberry asked.

"Lots of good stuff," I said. "We can talk when I get back."

"Great," Mulberry said, but I could hear a nervousness in his voice. "I talked with Dan. We're checking on blood samples for the victims who last remember being at Ivan's clubs."

"That will help, right?"

"While evidence of datura in their systems is a great first step, without any proof of where it's coming from or what exactly is in it besides datura, we don't really have a leg to stand on, legally that is. Like I told you before, this would be a brand new defense."

"Did Dan tell you his theory about the professor's records? How they are all in one place, safe from prying internet eyes?"

"Yeah," Mulberry said.

"Do you think he keeps them with him? Or locked up?" Mulberry didn't answer right away so I kept thinking aloud. "If I was him, and I'm obsessive about protecting this stuff, I think I'd keep those documents close to my research and locked up. You wouldn't want to drive around with them, what if you got into an accident?"

"I guess," Mulberry said, his voice wary. "When will you be back?"

I looked at the GPS. It predicted my arrival in Miami Beach in a little over two hours. "Not sure," I said. "I'll give you a call in a bit."

"Where are you going?" Mulberry asked.

"I'll call you later," I said and hung up, then pushed my foot onto the gas pedal sending the little Audi shooting forward and causing Blue to lose his balance, falling back against the seat. He gave me a disapproving look and repositioned himself. "Don't worry," I said. "I've got a plan."

CHAPTER SEVENTEEN
A PLAN... SORT OF

A plan was an exaggeration of what I had. What I had was an idea to go over to Professor Nablestone's research facility in the Everglades and see what I could see.

The turnoff was not marked, and I passed it twice before discovering the narrow driveway. The road was a mix of sand and shells, perhaps imported from the nearby beaches. A chain blocked the driveway about forty yards from the main road.

I got out and, finding it padlocked, left the car, continuing on foot with Blue. The day was hot and the Everglades still. The driveway was exposed to the sun, lined on both sides by tall grasses that swayed ever so slightly, apparently catching a breeze that refused to find me. The vibrations of crickets emerged from the grasses, the sounds rising and falling rhythmically.

A ten minute walk down the road and I began to doubt if I was going the right way. This facility had received millions of dollars in funding, you'd think they could afford a paved drive and an actual guard with a gatehouse. Every tiny little island in Miami seemed to have one. Maybe there was nothing here. Then again, maybe that's just what they wanted people to think.

Moments later, I spotted the roof of a structure beyond the grasses.

It came fully into view when the driveway opened into a parking lot. The building was on our right. It was two stories tall, fronting on the water with no windows on its back or the side wall facing me. It would have looked like a blank box except for the single door that lead out to the parking lot.

Cars were parked in the lot, their noses facing the water, bodies parallel to the building. Two Hondas, a Volvo, and a Corolla. I recognized the Volvo from the college's parking lot. It belonged to Dr. Nablestone's female TA. I walked up to it and peered into the driver's seat. She kept it neat and tidy.

Looking up at the building from this close to the water, I could see that large glass doors on both levels faced the Everglades. There was a balcony on the second floor that shaded several boat slips below. I heard a door open and a man stepped out onto the balcony.

"Hi," I called, waving to him. He approached the railing. "My car broke down right near the top of your driveway and I came down looking for a phone." I held up my cell phone which I'd turned off. "Mine's dead." I laughed. "If I had known what a far walk it was, I woulda just waited for someone to drive by."

It was hard to read his expression, the sun was behind him and I raised my free hand to block it, but the man's face remained in shadow. "I'll call a tow," the man said. "Return to your car."

He began to turn when I called out, "Do you think I could have a glass of water? It's awfully hot out here."

The man looked down at me. "Fine," he said. "I'll be right down."

I made my way toward the door in the side wall. Soon after, it opened and he waved for me to enter. "Thanks so much," I said. "You know, I wanted to see the Everglades but I didn't know how hot they would be." I turned around looking at the small waiting room we'd entered. A couple of chairs against one wall, an empty reception desk in front of a door that led deeper into the building. There was a key card swiper at just above waist height. The man pointed to a water cooler. I took a paper cup off the top and filled it. "Thanks again," I said before gulping down the water. "What is this place?" I asked, looking around, hoping I looked innocently confused. "At least it's nice and cool," I said referring to the air conditioning that kept the room at what felt like near freezing after the heat of my walk.

The man frowned. He looked to be in his late forties, dark hair, skin lined and tan from hours in the sun and wind. He was a couple of inches taller than me and broader. I could tell by the way he carried himself that he knew how to fight, nobody just naturally has that much balance. "Don't worry about it," he said, eyeing me. I turned and refilled my cup, sipping it slowly, trying to look like I didn't know how to fight. "You've had your water," he said and opened the door for me. The sun poured in. I felt it's heat.

"Right, sorry to keep you," I said, and walked out with the cup still in my hand.

"The tow truck will meet you at your car."

"Any chance you could give me a ride?" I asked, wiping sweat off my forehead. "It is really hot." He looked at me and then down at Blue. "Do you have a dog?" I asked.

The man nodded.

"It's hot for him, too," I said. "With that fur coat, in this weather."

Blue sat by my side, his tongue lolling out of his head, bouncing with each pant. I leaned over and gave him the water in my cup. He lapped at it and then looked up at the man in front of us with his best puppy dog stare.

"I can't right now," the man said. He looked toward the Everglades and I heard the whine of an airboat not far off.

"Do you do tours here?" I asked. "In airboats? I've seen the signs along the way."

The man didn't smile. "No," he said, and then closed the door on me.

Blue and I hiked back down the drive and when we got there, I found Sanjit's son waiting with a tow truck.

"Hey," I said.

"Oh, hi, how are you?" he asked. "Car trouble?"

"Not really," I answered and leaned against his truck. "Fuck, it's hot."

Sanjit's son wiped his brow with a well-worn bandana. "Yeah." He slapped at a mosquito that buzzed around us but missed. "Didn't you call for a tow?"

"Do you know what they do down there?" I asked him.

"Not sure. I've seen them out on their airboats. Research or something, collecting samples, right?" he asked.

I hadn't seen any airboats but I'd noticed the docks in the front of the building. "Samples of what?" I asked.

The boy shrugged again. "Plants and stuff. I don't know? Do you need a tow?" he asked again.

"No, I'm fine. But don't tell anyone, okay?"

"What do you mean?"

"Anyone asks, you gave me a tow, fixed my car, and sent me on my way."

"What was wrong with it?"

"With what?"

"Your car."

"Oh, I don't know. Make something up."

A smile crept onto his face. "Is this detective work?"

"Oh yeah."

"Is there a reward?"

"Definitely. Here," I pulled out a pen and paper from my glove compartment and wrote my cell number on it. "Text me if anyone calls asking about me. Also," I wrote down the Volvo's license plate and color. "Let me know if this car goes by you. Or if a hunter green Jag comes this way." I wrote that down on the paper, too. He took it from me. "Remember if anyone asks about me, tell them you sent me on my way. And don't tell them I'm a detective."

"You're undercover?" he whispered.

"Something like that," I answered.

"When do I get the reward?"

"Here," I pulled out two hundred dollar bills. "Consider this a down payment."

The boy grinned and jumped into his truck. I watched him pull out and head east.

Driving back toward Miami, I passed the casino and entered into the world where there were things besides gator bites, information, and gas to buy. I pulled into a large and full Walmart parking lot, stopping in the shade of a cart return center. Climbing out of the car, I motioned for Blue to join me. Looking across the rooftop of the cars, row after row of them, reflecting the sunlight back in shiny, painful spots of light, I squinted at the mother of all big box stores.

What a perfect name for those behemoths of American retailing. No need for imagination. Blue and I headed toward one of the entrances. The glass doors slid open and a whoosh of cool air came at us. We walked into a fluorescent-lit giant of a room. I stood for a moment on the threshold looking into the space. Gray walls, a ceiling so high that the designer could safely expose the ducts, wires and other innards, confident that no one would ever look up. A woman with dyed brown hair set in curls wearing a Walmart badge and a smile approached me.

"I'm sorry," she said with a smile that exposed a smear of red lipstick marring her front tooth, "we don't allow pets."

I smiled back at her and leaned in, creating an intimate space between the two of us in that big space. "You've got a little lipstick on your tooth," I said and pointed to my own front tooth.

She blushed and raised her lip, rubbing at the tooth with her index finger, the nail painted as red as her lips. "Thank you," she said with a smile. "I wonder how many people noticed and didn't say anything?" Her blush deepened.

I smiled at her. "It's a nice shade."

She smiled broadly, "Thank you."

Blue and I began to pass her and she followed us. "Oh, but, we don't allow pets."

I turned back to her. "He's a service dog. I have seizures."

The color from her earlier embarrassment drained from her face. "Oh," was all she said.

"Don't worry," I told her. "He will keep me safe." She nodded looking down at Blue. "Can you tell me where I'd find exercise clothing?"

She directed me to aisle 7b. First, I passed the prepared food area, a hint of fry in the air. Deeper into the box, I walked through the produce section and turned left at the potatoes. Aisle after aisle opened on either side of us as Blue and I walked down a corridor so long that I felt as if I was in a cartoon, where the distance never closes between Bugs Bunny and his destination.

The aisles opened up in the center and clothing was hung on racks that spread across an area which, if you came upon it in the forest, would seem like a magically large meadow. We wandered between the racks, passed synthetic suits and lacy frilled shorts to where the workout clothing hung. I found a pair of black leggings meant for jogging and was looking for clothing in my size, the metal hangers clicking against each other as I pushed them aside, when I glanced up and saw an aisle lined with camouflage gear.

Taking the leggings with me, I headed toward it. As I approached I could see a woman about twenty yards down the aisle, standing behind a waist high counter. She had gray hair, big owl glasses and a friendly smile. Behind her, hung on the walls in metal brackets, were guns. Long rifles and shot guns. Inside the case, lined up in neat shiny rows, were knives. I laid my hand on the glass, staring down at them. "Can I help you?" she asked.

I looked up at her and smiled. "Yes."

EK

After my shopping trip I drove back to a public launch I'd spotted down the road from the research center. I pulled off to the side so the car wasn't visible to passing traffic and out of the way of the boat launch.

Rolling down the windows, I turned off the car but it was like sitting in a metal box broiling in the sun. Putting the windows back up, I blasted the air. There seemed something almost disingenuous about sitting in the Audi, its navigation screen glowing, the wood paneling gleaming, and the leather, tawny and soft. I felt like an alien in my spaceship.

Why was I sitting here? Because of an instinct. Something in my gut that said something was going on there that was important. Hugh's freedom, the evidence necessary to reveal the true nature of this crime, was in that building. However, as the first hour passed into the second and I kept my phone turned off to avoid any calls or questions, I began to see that I was here because I needed this to end. I had to get Hugh clear before I blew up my life again.

As the sun set it sliced through the grasses with blades of bright orange. A pick-up truck pulled in. There were two guys in the truck and they were hauling an airboat. When they saw me, both of them frowned.

I waved to the men with a friendly smile and climbed out of the car, walking around the front. "Hi," I said.

The men nodded at me as they got out of the truck which they'd positioned so that the trailer holding the airboat's tires stopped just at the water line.

The man on the far side of the airboat spit on the ground, then moved his wad of chewing tobacco into his other cheek, looking at me over the cab of the truck. He wore a baseball cap low over his eyes. A brown ponytail, tangled and dull, came out the back.

The man standing nearer smiled at me. He wore a button-down shirt that strained against his bulging belly and a pair of cargo shorts. Gray hair puffed out from under a trucker cap that featured a bass on its brim. "The Everglades are a dangerous place. You should head back home."

"You guys are going out?" I asked.

He nodded. "Fishing."

The one with the chewing tobacco shook his head. "Come on, Carl," he said. "Let's go."

I put my hands up. "Sorry, didn't mean to bother you."

Carl turned to his friend and began to help him unstrap the airboat. It had a shallow draft, no more than a couple of inches. The bottom looked like stainless steel. The giant fan reminded me of hospitals in third world countries. Places where the air was so heavy you need a big ass fan to move it.

Carl jumped up and into the driver's seat, then his friend unlatched the last strap. The boat slipped quickly into the canal, its nose dipping under the water for a moment before resurfacing and bobbing gently. I leaned against my car hood; it was still hot from the day but the air was beginning to cool. A breeze blew through the grass from the west.

The other man climbed into the pickup truck, it was silver and shiny and looked brand new. In contrast, the airboat had red, cracked, pleather seats and a dinged up frame, rust and dirt coloring the fan a matte gray-brown. The tobacco-chewer pulled the truck up next to me, cut the engine and climbed out. He locked the vehicle with a beep and then walked to the shore where Carl started up the fan.

The fan chopped through the air slowly and the edge of the rectangular boat knocked gently against the cement of the launch. The truck driver turned back to look at me, then spit a wad of dark brown gunk onto the ground, just above the water line. "Be careful," he said in a gruff voice, then turned and stepped lightly onto the boat. As he took his seat next to Carl the fan picked up energy, cutting through the air so quickly I couldn't see the blade inside the cage, just a whirl of black, like a spinning disk. A roar accompanied the movement and the airboat shot away from the shore leaving a foaming wake behind it. They disappeared into the canals long before the sound of their fan engine faded.

When I got back into the car I checked my phone. The green Jaguar had arrived on the scene, the Volvo hadn't left. It appeared the whole gang would be there.

CHAPTER EIGHTEEN
EXECUTION

The croaking of the frogs started when the last liquid golden rays of sunlight blinked at the horizon and the sky softened into the dusty pink and blues of dusk. Pulling out the Walmart bags from the trunk, I rifled through them. I slipped the long, tight, black leggings on under my dress. Then, turning to face the grasses, I pulled my dress over my head and shrugged into the camouflage shirt, bringing the hood over my head, covering my hair and forehead. I kicked off my flats and put on black sneakers over a pair of black socks. Using the electric tape I covered the splashes of reflective material on the sneakers.

Clipping the utility belt around my waist, I secured a Jimmy Bar (the car breaking-into device favored by juvenile delinquents, at least when I was one) to my left hip. The gun Bobby had loaned me went into my new shoulder holster and I swung it around my back, looping my arms through. I pulled out my new knife, curved with a serrated tip and a camouflage handle. It came with a sheath that attached to the other side of my belt. The travel-size roll of duct tape fit into one of the belt's pockets. Lastly, I ripped open a package of cotton balls and pushed two into the crest of my breasts.

The night was growing darker and the single light above the launch flickered on, throwing long shadows. I tapped my thigh and Blue got into position. I checked the road and, seeing it empty, crossed. We were fully exposed as we walked over the short and narrow bridge toward the power towers. The white columns were lit up, and, by far, the largest, brightest thing for miles. But there was no one there to see us. Quickly we got onto the dirt road running parallel with the canal and highway.

We ran at a steady pace. Our footfalls on the dirt surface were not nearly as loud as the nocturnal creatures who remained invisible, hidden away in the grasses and trees. I knew the entrance to the facility was east of the next power station, so crossed back over onto the road there. It was still about another half mile and Blue and I ran quickly. I heard a car coming up behind us and, turning, saw two bright headlights closing in. I turned my head forward and raised my arms, palms flat, blocking my face as the car passed. Its red taillights were still visible in the distance when I got to the beginning of the research facility's driveway.

The shells crunched under my feet as I ran down the road. I heard an engine and stopped to listen. It was a fan boat. I picked up my pace again, straining to hear the sound of an approaching car over the mating calls of the creatures hidden in the darkness. The fear of a car coming and having to dip into the grasses, feeling the water of the Everglades against my calves and the wet grasses tickling my ankles, made me pick up my pace and soon the building was in sight.

I slowed and regained my breath as I approached the grassy parking lot. The same cars were there, plus the Jaguar.

There were no lights on the outside of the facility, its windowless facade stood out as a black box against the charcoal gray sky. A flash of lightning illuminated the clouds for a moment followed by the distant sound of thunder.

I skirted the grasses, pausing to hunker down in the shadows and pushed swabs of cotton into my nose. Breathing steadily through my mouth I crouched low and hurried up next to the Volvo, then peeked over the hood. I could see the front of the facility. There were five airboats tied to the dock, filling all the available slips.

It was quieter in the car but I could still hear the croaking of the bull frogs and the occasional gust of wind as it whipped through the grasses, making them whistle. Blue's ears perked and I strained to hear the sound of approaching footfalls. Keys jingled and the driver's side door unlocked with a click.

The blonde TA climbed in and threw two tote bags on the passenger seat with a sigh. Then she closed the driver's side door and put her key in the ignition. The headlights shot out into the Everglades, lighting the hammock of apple trees across the canal. Her radio came to life tuned to an 80's station that was playing Madonna's Like a Prayer. Before she put the car in reverse I sat up quickly, reaching my left arm over the headrest to grab the top of her head. Simultaneously I raised my right arm around her neck, pulling her throat hard against the seat with my forearm and resting the sharp blade of my knife against the flesh under her ear.

She squeaked.

"Quiet," I said.

Her eyes dashed to the rearview mirror. It was dark in the back of the car but I could see the terror in her eyes easily enough, huge and tearful.

"I am not going to hurt you as long as you tell me what I need to know. Are we clear?"

She blinked at me, confusion clouding the terror in her gaze.

"I need to know about the drugs you're making in there," I said. "I need to know where you keep the records."

"The records?" she said.

"Yes, the records, the information on what you're making."

She didn't answer so I pushed the knife against her neck a little harder, biting into the flesh below her ear. She squeezed her eyes shut. "You know what I'm talking about," I said.

She didn't respond. Braver than I thought. "Listen, if you don't give me the information I need I'll kill you because you will be useless to me. Do you understand?" She just blinked. "Nod if you understand. Oh right, sorry, I forgot. You can't nod."

She blinked again. "I'm going to take that as a yes, that you understand your situation. That I will kill you. However, I'm willing to bargain for your life. I'm willing to let you live as long as you tell me what I need to know. Do you understand me?"

She took a shuddering breath through her mouth. "On Professor Nablestone's computer, in his safe."

"Where is the safe?"

"In his office."

"What is the code?"

"I don't know. He's in there right now, why don't you go ask him?" She had spunk. And I kinda liked it.

"Get undressed," I told her.

EK

I left her taped up in the reeds by her car with Blue watching over her. "If you try to escape, he'll rip your face off," I told her. "If I get caught and he either sees me leave or I'm not back within the hour, he'll rip your face off. Do you understand?" She nodded, the skin around her cheeks bulging against the silver duct tape. "Do you have anything else you need to tell me?" I asked. She shook her head no.

Her skirt suit almost fit me, though it was a bit baggy. However, my utility belt helped hold it up. With the lab coat over my shoulder holster and buttoned to cover the belt buckle, my face blocked by a baseball cap I found in her car I could pass on CCTV cameras. Hopefully, the blonde, whose name I'd learned was Julia, had told me the truth. Inside were two security guards and five other medical researchers. Hopefully I wouldn't run into any of them. For them, not me.

I walked over to the front door and swiped her keycard against the entrance. It opened with a click and beep. The light was on in the small waiting room I'd seen earlier. Passing through to the next door I swiped the key card again and entered into a hallway with linoleum floors and fluorescent lights running the length of it. I only passed one door on my way to the elevator and it stayed solidly closed as I pushed the up button.

There was a thump from a door down the hall and I turned toward it, my heart rate climbing as adrenaline fueled my system. The banging came again and I saw one of the doors rattle in its frame. As the elevator doors opened I stood back, the brim of my hat covering most of my face. I watched the ground, waiting to see feet. But it was empty. Another thump down the hall and I stepped quickly into the elevator, pressing the button for the second floor, keeping my gaze down. Feeling the lens of the CCTV camera on the back of my neck.

According to Julia, Professor Nablestone's office was the second door on the left when I got out. The door was fake wood and a small plaque next to it identified the occupant. Unbuttoning the lab coat, I pulled out the gun, holding it lightly in my left hand. Reaching out with my right, I tried the knob, and it opened right up.

The room was large and square with sliding glass doors that opened onto a wooden deck. As I walked in lightning flashed behind the dark clouds that filled the sky. The grasses and low trees stretching across the land looked like a bulging carpet of blackness. The shallow waters weaving through them shone bright silver for just a second before disappearing into darkness again. Professor Nablestone was sitting at his desk, a lamp illuminating his work area. He looked up from his keyboard and seeing me in the doorway, started. "Keep your hands where I can see them," I said as I closed the door behind me with my foot.

He held them up. "How can I help you?" he asked.

"Open your safe."

"What safe?"

I smiled. "Let's not play games. Open the safe."

"Or you'll shoot me?"

He didn't look afraid. I had a feeling this wasn't the first time he'd had a gun aimed at his head before. "Yes," I said. "I thought the threat was implied."

"You'd never make it out of here."

"Why would you care? You'll be dead."

He laughed.

I walked toward him and grabbing him by the collar, hauled him out of his seat and toward the closet. He followed me, his hands still up. I dropped him on the ground and opened the closet door. Pointing to the safe in the wall I demanded that he open it.

He smiled and, pushing off the floor, stood. I held my gun on him as he maneuvered into the small space. Nablestone opened the safe and began to reach into it. I saw him hesitate, a twitch in his shoulder. Quicker than average but not quick enough to catch me, he turned, extending his fingers, and with a puff of air from between pursed lips, blew white powder into my face. I knocked his hand down, grabbed the back of his neck and pulled him into a kiss. I felt him take a sharp intake of breath as our lips pressed together, his dry and open just a hair, mine moist and firmly closed. When I pulled away his eyes were glassy. I wiped my lips with the back of my hand. "I was hoping you might try something like that," I said. He didn't respond.

"Get me the laptop, I want all your research notes, every little dirty secret."

He turned around and reaching into the safe pulled out a laptop encased in what looked like military-grade protection. I took it from him. "What else should I take?" He shook his head, standing aside to show me the empty safe. "How long until that stuff wears off you?"

"About ten minutes," he answered.

"That quick?"

"Yes."

"Do you have more?"

"Yes."

"Different kinds?"

He smiled. "So many different uses."

"Are they here?"

"Yes, downstairs."

I thought about making him take me down there and give them to me but figured I had enough. No reason to be reckless.

"Escort me out," I said. "If anyone tries to stop us, you tell them I'm okay. Do whatever you have to in order for me to make it out safe."

"Yes," he said.

We left the office, Professor Nablestone walking beside me down the hall. Waiting for the elevator I asked him. "Did you kill Lawrence Taggert?"

"No," he said.

"Did you make Hugh Defry do it?"

"Yes," he said, a smile drifting across his face. "It was perfect."

The elevator doors opened and the man who'd refused me a ride earlier was standing there. "Evening," he said, and began to step out of the elevator. Professor Nablestone walked in but as I passed the guard he looked at me more closely. "Hey," he said, and grabbed my arm. The elevator door dinged and began to close but Professor Nablestone held it open. "It's okay, Gravy, she's with me. We're leaving."

He glared at me and then looked over at Professor Nablestone. "Who is this, sir?"

He looked over at me. "I don't know," he answered. "But she knows about Taggert."

"Taggert? Sir?"

I pulled my arm free. "Yes, Taggert. Clearly above your clearance."

The door began to close again but this time it was Gravy who stopped it. "Let us go," Professor Nablestone said.

"I'll escort you out, Sir."

"That's not necessary," I said, but he got into the elevator and pushed the door close button.

"No problem," he said. "How's your car?"

I didn't answer him. Professor Nablestone stared at the doors and when they opened he walked out first. "Thanks for loaning me your car," I said to him. He looked over at me, his expression blank. "Give me your keys," I said.

Gravy walked with us down the hall and watched with suspicion as his boss handed over the keys to the Jaguar. I went to open the door to the waiting room but it was locked. Swiping the key card across the pad released it but Gravy grabbed my arm as I pushed through. He snatched the key card out of my hand and stared down at it, reading the name across the top. I twisted my body, bent my knees, and rammed my palm into the bridge of his nose, hard enough to break it but not enough to kill him.

His head flew back, blood spewing up toward the ceiling. I snatched back the key card and pushed through to the waiting room, swiped the card, and broke through to the outside. The air was moist and it was dark. A strong wind blew from the west bringing the smell of storm with it.

CHAPTER NINETEEN
RACING IN REEDS

I ran across the lot to Professor Nablestone's car and unlocked it. The orange of the parking lights flashed across the dark landscape. Jumping into the driver's seat I threw the laptop into the passenger seat well. Backing out I saw, in the red glow of my reverse lights, that the building door was still closed. Switching into drive I passed the other cars, stopping at Julia's Volvo. My headlights caught her figure, wrists and ankles bound, wearing my black leggings and camouflage top, her blonde hair peeking from under the hood, duct tape stretched from cheek to cheek. Blue stood by her side, hackles raised, teeth bared, pupils reflecting red in the harsh headlights.

I leaned across the passenger seat and opened the door. Blue saw me and, lowering his ears and tail, leapt into the seat. I pulled the door shut and, looking up, saw Gravy standing in the doorway, a walkie talkie in his hand. I started down the driveway toward the highway with the headlights off, hearing the crunch of the shells beneath the tires. Seeing the twinkle of lights ahead, I braked.

"All right, Blue," I said. "We're going in."

I opened my door and motioned for him to jump over me. He leapt, his fur coat brushing against my nose. The lights I'd seen were now two clear headlights, coming quickly our way. I reached into the well of the passenger seat and grabbed the handle of the laptop case. Staying low I took my foot off the brake and twisted out of the car, joining Blue in the reeds.

As we inched into the thick growth my feet sank deeper beneath the water. The grasses scratched against the lab coat and tickled my cheeks. The sounds of nocturnal creatures were louder in the brush. Lightning flashed and the pitter patter of rain began. Blue followed me closely, his nose brushing the back of my calf, reassuring me of his presence, and himself of mine.

As we came out to a canal, I heard a car engine stop on the road behind us. "She must have gone into the swamp," I heard one man say. I motioned for Blue to go into the canal first. He stepped forward and sank into the black water, his legs pumping and tail swinging back and forth. He crossed the canal and climbed into a hammock of apple trees. I stood on the bank, not wanting to go further into the dark water, not knowing how deep it was or what was down there.

The sound of another engine and men's voices urged me on. I stepped forward. holding the laptop above my head and preparing to tread water, but my sneakers touched the bottom when I was submerged up to my chest. The water was warm and I could feel grasses gliding against my bare calves, slithering under my skirt and around my knees. I held my breath as I waded across the canal. Blue growled and I froze, following his gaze.

Small beady eyes rested on top of the water, the hint of a tail close behind. A juvenile alligator. It watched me from ten feet away. I let my breath out slowly, staring at it, waiting for it to make its move. But it just watched me until the sound of men's voices grew louder, then without even the whisper of a splash it ducked beneath the surface.

I lunged for the hammock where Blue crouched. Pushing the laptop up between two trunks, I grabbed at the exposed roots and pulled myself up onto the dry bed of decaying leaves. I picked up the laptop and then followed Blue through the tangle of trunks. Pulling off the lab coat and dragging myself between the narrow spaces, pushing the laptop ahead of me, I didn't feel the rain anymore. But when I turned back to look at the water it was dappled with rings of disturbance.

I heard the engine of an airboat start. It sounded far away. Blue and I pulled deeper into the hammock, gathering the darkness around us. The air was wet and heavy, smelling of bark and dirt. The airboat got closer and I gripped a tree trunk watching. Was it the professor and his minions or some fishermen like the ones I'd met earlier? The airboat's engine slowed as it approached and I pulled my knife out, holding it loosely in my hand, ready to use it and the forbidding terrain to my advantage.

The engine stopped entirely and I saw the fan boat drift into view. Laughter rose above the sound of the rain and I took a chance, stepping forward to get a better view. I recognized Carl and his tobacco-chewing friend. A flashlight beam cut through the grasses. I slunk back into the trees.

The two fisherman turned to look at the approaching light. It danced through the reeds and then stopped, centering on the fishermen.

"What are you doing here?" a voice asked.

"I'd ask you the same thing," Carl said. "You wandering around in the reeds?" He was holding his hand up to block the light from his eyes.

"Did you see a woman wearing a white lab coat?"

Both men laughed. "Yeah," Carl said, his voice breathless. "And she was walking an alligator." This brought on a new wave of laughter.

I heard another airboat engine start up in the distance. The light jerked off the men and into the stand of trees, barely penetrating past the first row of trunks. "How long have you been here?" the man with the flashlight asked.

"Just arrived," Carl answered. "We would have got here sooner if we'd known there was a lab-coated woman on the loose." They started laughing again and I wondered if perhaps there was a bit of drinking going along with their fishing.

"The woman is dangerous. Do not approach her."

Their laughter faltered. "Hey, now, what's going on?" Carl asked.

"Perhaps you two should head in for the night. Looks like a storm is coming."

The flashlight turned back into the grasses and I watched its glow as it headed toward the driveway.

"Well, what do you think of that?" Carl's friend asked.

"Think it has anything to do with that lady we saw?" Carl answered as I worked my way back to the canal.

"She wasn't wearing a lab coat," his friend pointed out as I stepped up to the water's edge.

"But ain't it awful weird?"

"Hey," I whispered.

Neither of the men turned. Carl was doing something with a fishing rod and the other man was sipping from a small silver decanter that the rain pinged off of as he raised it to his mouth. "I guess you're right," the friend agreed.

"Think she was dangerous?" Carl asked, looking up from his hook.

The other man gestured with his canteen toward the reeds. "I'd say that guy was dangerous."

"Excuse me," I said louder.

They both turned. I waved. They squinted against the darkness. "Hi," I said. "Can you give me a lift?"

Carl dropped the rod he was working on and it fell to the boat's floor with a rattle. The other man froze, the silver decanter paused just before his lips.

I came out of the grove further and with a wide step alighted onto their boat. Blue followed closely behind me. They both continued to stare. "Please take me back to the launch."

The steady whine of approaching airboats hummed in the air. "We better go," I said.

Lightning flashed across the sky and thunder sounded quickly after. A gust of wind whipped down the canal, rustling the leaves of the apple trees into a blur. A giant, white spotlight lit up the canal behind us, cutting through the protective darkness. "Boys, we need to go now," I said.

"Now wait here a minute," Carl said. "We don't want any trouble."

"You've already got it. Now you need to start up that engine or the people on that boat will probably kill you, and if they keep you alive they'll probably frame you for my murder so," I made a pushing motion with my hands, "let's go."

The other airboat was slowly going down the canal, its spotlight scanning the grasses on the one side and then the apple trees on the other. Carl opened his mouth to speak again but the other man, the one whose name I still didn't know, interrupted. "I think we better go," he said, his eyes watching the purposeful scanning of the approaching light. Carl bent down and secured his fishing rod to the hull.

"Now," I said, urgency in my voice.

"I'm going, I'm going," Carl said, jumping into his seat. I sat on one of the free chairs and clutched the laptop case and lab coat across my lap. Blue hunkered down at my feet, pressing his back against my legs. The fan whirled to life and the boat smoothly glided forward. Carl kept at an easy pace, continuing down the canal, away from the searching light until the hammock of apple trees ended.

Lightning crackled as we entered a field that existed both above and below water. Grasses, some tall, others low, still more beneath the water, shifted with the wind, whipping back and forth. The surface of the water blurring with each gust. My hair, wet from the rain, clung to my face and wrapped itself around my neck.

As we raced across the grasses, barreling through the tall and skimming over the short, I blinked against the rain drops. Another airboat mounted with a spotlight shot out from behind a hammock of apple trees and flew across the water toward us. I looked back at Carl. His jaw tensed before hurling a loogie overboard, the wind taking it the moment it left his mouth.

A voice over a loudspeaker hailed us from the encroaching boat. "Stop please," it said.

"Well, ain't that polite," Carl yelled over the airboat's engine.

"This is the police, stop now," the voice said with authority.

Carl slowed down. "What are you doing?" I yelled over my shoulder at him.

"Don't worry," he yelled back. "This isn't my first time at the rodeo."

As the second boat approached all I could see was the light. When they were about ten yards away Carl throttled the fan up to high and we shot off across the open landscape. The other boat pursued us, their light blazing over our stern, casting strange and frightening shadows through the fan. As it began to gain on us, Carl turned the boat hard, the bow submerging for a moment, and the stern spun around 180 degrees. We jerked forward and passed the other boat as they sped by us.

Their light blinded me for a moment. Now they knew I was aboard. But suddenly that didn't matter all that much as Carl was headed full speed toward a stand of tall grasses. He hit them hard, crushing the long stems. I turned around and saw them pop back up behind us.

For a moment we were totally surrounded by the swaying reeds, only a small patch of turbulent sky above us. Then we we were out of them and into another canal lined on one side with trees and on the other with grasses. Carl turned the rudder hard just before we slammed into the apple trees and we took off down the narrow passage. I turned around and watched as the other boat flew out of the grasses and slammed into the apple hammock across the way. The light jerked out and the scene fell into darkness. Our fan engine's furious whirling was the only thing I could hear. "Woohoo," Carl yelled. "Haha, we showed those bastards, didn't we, Earl?"

Earl nodded, his forehead creased. Then he raised the flask to his lips. Carl slowed the boat, quieting the engine as we navigated through canals cut between the reeds, which seemed to reach for us as they bent in the wind. We took a left into a canal cut through more apple hammocks. The wind whistled through the tops of the trees, at water level barely a breeze was felt. Carl slowed and then cut the engine. I strained to listen, hearing the sound of rain tinging against the hull, the croaking of the bull frogs, Blue panting, but no other airboats.

Carl spit into the water again and then started the engine back up and puttered us slowly forward until I could see the launch. A car drove by on the road as Carl tapped the boat against the cement and Earl jumped onto solid land.

CHAPTER TWENTY
BLANK

I ran because something terrifying was following me. Branches grabbed at my arms, roots hooked my feet. Blue kept nudging my hip, telling me to fight on.

I blinked my eyes. Blinding light. I blinked again, began to see shapes, dark and light, browns, blacks and whites. "Sydney," I heard someone say. I could feel scratches on my legs from the trees, they burned.

"Sydney," I heard again, the voice concerned, soft and hopeful.

A pressure on my left shoulder made my head loll toward it. I heard the shuffling of bodies moving around a room. I blinked my eyes again, but they wouldn't stay open, only offering the briefest glimpse of a world made up of shadow figures. I rested for a moment, confused, feeling lightheaded.

Taking a deep breath I forced my eyes open. A dark figure closed in on me, the white light behind it making its edges glow brown. "Sydney," it said. "Can you hear me?"

"Who are you?" I asked, my tongue felt heavy and my voice sounded small.

"It's me, Sydney. It's Mulberry."

The name meant nothing to me.

There was a couch in front of me. Hugh and Santiago were sitting on it, talking to each other, not looking over at me. I was sitting in a chair. There were slippers on my feet. Hugh was looking at me now. His mouth moved. "Sydney?"

It felt like my brain lurched. Like from a train car pile up. My vision twisted and stayed blurred for a moment. Movement and then Hugh and Santiago were over me, their faces close. I could smell shampoo and black pepper. "Can you hear me?" Hugh asked, his voice tight.

"Yes," I said, the world sliding back into place. There was a ceiling above me. Santiago and Hugh looked at each other. I must have fallen out of the chair, I thought.

"I'll get the doctor," Santiago said.

Hugh nodded then turned his attention back to me. Santiago rose off his knees, using the upholstered chair I'd been sitting in for leverage. "Sydney, do you know who I am?" Hugh asked.

"Hugh?"

"Yes!"

"Hugh? What's going on?" I asked, lifting my head, raising a shoulder and propping myself up on an elbow. Behind Hugh was the couch I'd seen when I first opened my eyes. It was upholstered in red and gold with a straight back and low arms. Meant for visiting, not for relaxing. In front of it a low square table had an array of magazines fanned across it. Hugh's eyes twitched back and forth, he looked nervous. "What is it?" I asked as the first prickles of warning began to travel up my neck. Footsteps in the hall. Blue's growl hummed.

A door opened and I sat up further, peeking around the chair I'd slipped out of, to look at two approaching figures. It was Santiago and a woman wearing scrubs. There was a furrow between her brows and her lips were pursed. She moved quickly but loudly, her movements overemphasized. She bent over and grabbed the armrest of the chair then lowered onto her knees with a grimace of pain. Blue's growl clicked off and she asked. "Do you know your name?"

"Sydney Rye."

"That's good." She smiled, her face relaxing. Oh shit, I thought. When knowing your own name is an accomplishment something has gone terribly wrong.

I started to get up, climbing onto my hands and knees. The woman put a strong hand around my arm to help me. I took a breath there, looking down at my hands. The nails were filed and buffed. The skin littered with fresh pink scars, almost healed. I was wearing a sweatshirt and a pair of jeans with what felt like an elastic waist.

Sitting back onto my heels I felt my muscles move and a dull ache, as if I'd done a serious session of squats the day before. Aching but strong. Straightening my back I felt the vertebrae line up, my shoulders fall into place, my head raising to rest comfortably on my neck. It all worked.

I felt an itch and the sting of healing flesh on my left forearm. Pulling up my sleeve I found a long scar, small pieces of scab still pulling at the skin. I heard a click and Blue's growl rose again. A cool breeze touched me, and I watched as goosebumps rose around the wound. Looking up I saw an air conditioning vent, air humming out of it. "Where is Blue?" I asked.

"He's with Merl, totally safe," Hugh said.

"Not here?" I asked, listening to the air conditioner and not hearing Blue anymore.

"Let's get you up off the ground," the nurse said. She helped me into the chair and I was facing the couch again. Hugh and Santiago hovered around me. "Sit down," she told them. "Give her some room."

They complied, returning to their seats. The woman put a blood pressure cuff around my bicep. The velcro sounded like a strong wind tearing through trees.

The nurse looked up from my elbow, her stethoscope in her ears. The door was opening and a man wearing a white doctor's coat walked in. He was about six feet tall with salt and pepper hair. The man turned to Hugh and Santiago. "Could you two wait outside?" he asked.

They looked at each other. Santiago bit his lip and Hugh looked back at me, his eyes pleading. "I want them to stay," I said.

He nodded and then pulled up a chair made of dark wood with a padded seat. The nurse stood up and backed away. "Her vitals are good," she told him.

"Good," he said, sitting down. His pants raised up over his ankles exposing colorful socks. He smiled at me. "My name is Dr. Jose Garcia." The doctor folded his hands in his lap and leaned back. "Do you know who you are?"

"Yes," I answered.

"Do you know who I am?"

"Dr. Jose Garcia."

He nodded. "Good. Before I ask you any more questions, first I want to make it clear to you that you are in a safe place. No one can get to you here. Not only are you safe here, but so are your secrets."

The tingle of warning brushed the back of my neck again. "Am I a prisoner?" I asked.

The doctor shook his head. "No, no. Nothing you tell me will leave this room, doctor-patient privilege. There is no way I can end up in a court room." I glanced at Hugh and Santiago, but they were whispering to each other.

"Where am I?"

The doctor smiled again and separated his hands, resting them on his knees and leaning forward. "You're in Miami at the FGI headquarter's recovery department and I've been looking after you since your arrival here."

I felt an empty click inside my brain when I tried to remember. It felt the same as when a gun hammer taps an empty barrel. Terrifying when unexpected.

"How long have I been here?" I asked.

"You've been unresponsive for eighteen days."

"Excuse me?"

"While I'm sure you have lots of questions I'd like to take a look at your eyes real quick if that's okay." He pulled a small flashlight out of his breast pocket.

"Why?" I asked.

"To check the dilation. They look pretty good from here, but I'd like to take a closer look. It won't hurt. Just a little look."

I glanced at Hugh. He nodded.

"Okay," I said, my knuckles tightening on the arm rest.

The doctor leaned forward and took a firm grasp of my head. Using his thumb he pulled up my left eyelid and flashed his tiny light into it. I felt my pupil react, tightening inside the iris. He moved on to my right eye and did the same move then sat back smiling. "Very good," he said. "Now, can you tell me when you came to Florida?"

"Yes," I answered, remembering the flight with Mulberry. Landing in Miami. Seeing Hugh again after all these years.

"When was that?"

"I don't know. Feels like a week or so ago but obviously, if what you've said is true, then that's impossible."

He nodded. "So what is the last thing you do remember?"

Images flipped through my mind like index cards in a library file cabinet. Running along the driveway, crunching of shells under foot. Stepping into the professor's office, the brush of our lips, the glaze in his eyes. The way his mind fell blank. "Oh my God," I whispered.

"What?" Jose asked, "Do you see something?"

"No, I just...I was drugged."

"You remember?"

"No," I closed my eyes. Running into the reeds, (tick), wind whipping my face as we raced across the water, (click), the roar of the fan, (tap), the thunk of the boat against the cement launch.

"Do you remember going to Walmart?" Dr. Garcia asked me.

I looked up at him, remembering the knife's serrated edge. "I don't know," I lied.

He smiled. "That's fine. We'll see what comes back to you in the next couple of hours. Maybe you should just lie down and rest."

I looked over at Hugh and Santiago. "Can I have a minute with her before she lies down?" Hugh asked.

"Maybe I could ask you some questions, Doctor?" Santiago said, standing up and gesturing toward the door.

The doctor stood, dropping his flashlight back into his jacket pocket. "Just a moment." He looked down at me. "She needs to rest.'

Santiago opened the door and Dr. Garcia went through, followed by the nurse. Hugh watched the door close and then stood up and came around to give me a hug. It felt nice to have his arms around me. "Listen," he whispered. "Malina will come for you tonight."

"What?"

"Shh, quiet," his voice against my ear. "I love you. Thank you. I'll see you again soon." He squeezed me and I closed my eyes, squeezing back, knowing that he was on my side.

EK

I was in a bed now, my eyes closed, my head on a pillow. I heard that empty click as I tried to remember beyond the airboat reaching the launch. Blue's face, his muzzle blood-soaked, spatters up to his ears, his chest bright red, flashed across my vision. Blue's teeth were bared, his eyes telling me to run.

I sat up, gulping air, throwing the blankets off of me.

How much time had passed?

I was sitting in the forest, a lit cigarette between my lips, the smoke floating across my vision. I inhaled, feeling the acrid fumes fill my lungs, satiating a need there. Releasing the breath, smoke billowed from my mouth.

Blue sat next to me, one ear up straight, the other swiveling like a satellite. The ground was dry beneath me, but the air was moist and heavy. I could hear rain beating against the leaves. We were deep in the canopy. The lightning that flashed barely lit the dark interior. But the thunder seemed to vibrate the entire growth. Blue stood, his hackles rising, both ears straining forward.

He turned to look at me, his eyes calming, the whirl of the fan boat far away. They could not find us here. The fur on his muzzle was matted with blood up to his eyes. His chest was a mess of leaves and dirt, sticky and congealed looking. Lightning struck close, filling the air with its electric current. Sparks ignited the dried leaves and a fire quickly bloomed in the near distance, its flickering tongues dancing toward us.

Blue barked. I jumped up, taking the cigarette from between my lips and dropping it to the ground, grinding it out with my sneaker. He nudged me and barked again. I began to run away from the fire, pushing between the close trees, which seemed to pull at me, scraping my skin. I looked down and blood dripped off my elbow. I watched as a branch reached out and curled around my arm, squeezing the flesh. Blue barked again and I tried to pull away from it but another limb curled around my waist, pulling me against the trunk.

I struggled but felt weak and useless, my body exhausted. A branch wound around my chest, I reached down and bit at it, sinking my teeth through the bark into the sap. It grunted. I could feel its heartbeat through the bark against my back. Its breath was on my ear, it was whispering to me.

EK

"It's me," the voice said. "Mulberry. Joy, it's me, shhh..."

I looked down at myself and saw two arms holding me tight, one of them had a vicious bite wound on the forearm.

They were Mulberry's arms. His chest was against my back. I slumped as the adrenaline left my system in a rush. If Mulberry hadn't been gripping me I would have fallen. He picked me up easily. Holding under my knees and shoulders, Mulberry carried me back to the bed. After laying me down he stood over me, his brow knit, eyes scanning, looking for some kind of answer. He wrapped my right hand between both of his. "You recognize me?" he asked.

"Yes."

He laughed and seemed to choke on it, turning his face away from me and toward the closed curtains. They covered the left wall, blocking out all light except for a glow at the bottom where the thick drapes brushed against the wood floor.

"Did I bite you?" I asked, looking at the raw wound on his arm. He was wearing a white button-down shirt with the sleeves rolled up. It was wrinkled, and the front slightly untucked out of his gray slacks from our struggle.

Mulberry cleared his throat. "Yes," he said, turning his eyes back to me. "It's fine though. What did you see?"

I leaned back against the pillow feeling exhaustion overwhelm me. "He saved my life," I said.

"Who?" Mulberry asked.

I let my eyes slide shut. Mulberry raised his hand to my face and rubbed the edge of his thumb down my jaw line.

"Stay," I said. "Don't leave me." I realized for the first time in a long time that I didn't want to be alone. Not anymore.

"Okay," Mulberry said.

When I woke again sunlight streamed in through a gap in the curtains, creating a line of light across the room. Mulberry slept in a chair next to me, his hand over mine. His head was thrown over the back of the chair. I watched his Adam's apple bob as he swallowed in his sleep. Mulberry hadn't shaved in a couple of days. His beard was peppered with silver, copper, and gold.

The laptop. I suddenly remembered gripping it to my chest, squeezing it so that the edges of the case dug into my skin.

Mulberry's eyes fluttered and he looked over at me. Seeing me awake he smiled and sat up. "Hey," he said, leaning toward me.

"What about the laptop?" I asked.

He grinned.

"Did I give it to you?"

"We found it with you."

"What do you mean? Found me?"

Mulberry's brow furrowed and he brought both of his hands to hold mine. I remembered the wet, stringy pieces of grass as they swirled around my ankles, the water soaking through my sneakers, making them heavy and cold. I felt water seeping through my clothing, a wet chill flowing up my back. I shivered and Mulberry squeezed my hand. "It's still happening," I whispered.

"What?" He leaned forward.

"I don't know."

"Are you hallucinating? Is there something in the room?"

"I don't know," I said, pulling his hand to my breast, holding it close to me. "Maybe they are memories or maybe they are dreams."

"Like when you were fighting me?"

"I thought you were a tree." He nodded, looking concerned. "I was wearing cotton in my nose." I strained to remember. "Did I take it out?"

Mulberry frowned. "Professor Nablestone had developed a formula that went in through the eyes. It's only potent in the air for a short time and is fired from a gun, giving the assailant enough distance so that he's not affected. Once the victim is intoxicated the shooter can move in within three minutes."

My memory was beginning to clear. I had hugged and thanked Carl and Earl at the dock, then made my way back to my car. Nablestone must have found the car and been waiting for me.

"So he got me?" I asked, a tremble in my voice.

"No," Mulberry answered.

"What do you mean?" I turned to him, almost knowing what he was going to say.

"Professor Nablestone is dead."

"I killed him?"

Mulberry shook his head. "Blue did."

I nodded.

"I found him by the Audi. Blue tore his throat out."

"I remember Blue being covered in blood," I said. "Or I dreamed it."

"He was matted with blood when we found you," Mulberry said.

I didn't know whether it made me feel better or worse that my nightmare might have been a memory. "What about Hugh's case?"

"With the evidence from the laptop you managed to hold onto the entire time you were out there…" He smiled. "Only you," he laughed.

"What?"

He shook his head, smiling. "We had more than enough to prove Hugh was drugged."

"What do you mean?"

"It was all there, Sydney. Professor Nablestone kept meticulous notes of the whole thing. Lawrence was providing Ivan with one of Professor Nablestone's formulas, for the girls to use on johns. Nablestone found out. He thought it jeopardized his research and decided to take care of it."

"Out where?" I asked. Mulberry frowned in confusion. "Where did you find me? Where did I hold onto the laptop case?"

"The doctor didn't tell you?" I shook my head. "In the Everglades, Sydney. You were out there for almost thirty-six hours before we found you. You've been here for eighteen days. Completely pliable. Nothing of yourself in your eyes. It was terrifying."

I stared at him, my mind stuttering in place, unable to make sense of what he was saying. "But Hugh is free?" I asked. Mulberry nodded. "Did Robert know about it?"

"It looks pretty clear Nablestone acted alone."

"Was this the first time he'd done it?" I asked.

Mulberry shook his head. "Doesn't look that way. Dan found a few cases that could be connected. He sent all the information to the prosecutor."

"But so Hugh is free?" I asked.

Mulberry nodded. "Don't you remember seeing him?"

"Yes," I nodded. "Yes, I did. I remember. What about Ivan?"

"What about him?" Mulberry asked

"Is he going to jail?"

Mulberry shrugged. "That's up to the prosecutor. I'm sure they are starting an investigation." I felt anger rising in my chest and looked toward the window. "That's something—" Mulberry was cut off when the door opened.

He looked over his shoulder, nodded and leaned over me, kissing my forehead gently. "I'll be back in the morning," he promised.

"Where are you going?" I asked.

He smiled. "*Defry's* is reopening tonight. Hugh invited us."

"Us?"

"Yes us," Robert Maxim answered as he walked over to the curtains. He threw them apart letting the glow of sunset fill the room. I felt my pupils retract against the light. "We haven't much time," he said, turning back to us, his face in shadow. "And I'd like a moment alone before we go."

Bobby Maxim stood next to my bed looking down at me after Mulberry left. The setting sun cast long shadows across his face. He was staring at my bare leg where I'd thrown it over the blanket. His gaze flicked to my face. "I'm glad to see you awake. You gave us all a scare."

I sat, pushing myself up the bed while covering my leg with the sheet. He handed me a controller and I used it to raise the mattress into a sitting position. I felt mentally exhausted but my body didn't hurt. Except for the itch on my forearm and a low level of pain vibrating in my head I appeared to be in working order. "You feel strong?" Bobby asked as if reading my mind. He sat in the chair, pulling it around so that we faced each other.

"Strong?" I asked.

"We've had you on a real regimen here. Working out every day. Eating right. You were the perfect patient."

"I suppose you prefer me that way," I said.

"I knew you'd be back. You're a survivor," he said with a smile.

I nodded. "Did you know about Professor Nablestone?"

Bobby frowned. "In what way?"

"Let's start with any knowledge of his existence."

"Yes."

"You knew about his research?"

Robert nodded.

"And yet, it didn't occur to you that would be helpful to our investigation."

"I forgot about him," Bobby said. I laughed, closing my eyes and letting the humor bubble up inside of me. "I'm glad you find me amusing, Ms. Rye, but the truth is I didn't know he was behind this." I laughed harder, keeping my eyes closed.

Bobby stayed silent and when I wiped the tears from my eyes and looked over at him, he was smiling.

"You supported his research. You gave him money," I said, a hiccup of laughter in my voice.

"He was close with Lawrence's wife whom I've known for years." Robert smiled. "We dated in the 80s. But, I don't really think you want to know about my past love life. You want to know if I set this up in some way to lure you here. And the answer is no. You know me, Sydney," he leaned back in his chair. "Would I ever risk exposure in this way? I'm not an idiot."

I laughed again, not caring if it was truth or lies leaving his lips. "Is this another case of one of your knights running wild?" I asked, the mirth leaving my voice, a deep unsettling sensation roiling in my gut.

Bobby narrowed his eyes just a touch, a slight show of surprise.

That's when I realized Robert Maxim was where the lightning came from. He was the storm of violence I could not escape. The power of Maxim and his kind reached across the globe and into untold billions of lives. Allowing things to happen, not stopping corruption at its root. Thinking money and power were more important than kindness and compassion. The realization seared across my brain accompanied by a roll of thunder.

"What do you mean?" he asked me. "My knight?"

"From chess," I answered, the deep rumble fading from my ears. "Or would you have considered Professor Nablestone more of a pawn? Kurt Jessup must have at least been a bishop when he went rogue, killing my brother."

"I thought you didn't play chess."

"I lied."

He smiled and then laced his fingers together into a steeple. "Hugh is free," he said. I nodded. "Have you thought about my offer?"

"To have my own department with as many *guests* as I want?"

"You remember." He held eye contact.

"Do I have to live in Miami?" I asked.

I saw a glimmer of hope in the man's eyes. "You can live wherever you want. We have offices all over the world." He chuckled, "I could see you in Australia, Sydney."

"Is FGI buying the drugs that Professor Nablestone was developing?"

He smiled. "Can't you see how in the right hands it could be very useful?" Robert leaned toward me, resting his hands on the edge of my bed. "You used it, against him, didn't you?"

I sat forward. "I'm not afraid of you," I said.

He cocked his head.

"You can't kill me because I am an idea. That's why you need me." I leaned even closer, raising a hand out and resting it onto his shoulder. His cologne filled my nose and I enjoyed the mix of sandalwood and salt water. "Maybe I'll let you have me," I whispered so that my breath shook the strands of hair around his ears.

He turned to me and our lips almost touched. I felt the slimy reeds of the Everglades trail along my arms. Goosebumps followed. "You can die." Robert brought his hand up to my throat, closing his fingers around my neck. "But I know you don't fear death. Coming back to life would be your problem."

He let go of my throat and sat back. "I know you're still not well. It's unclear when you will be. But I am a patient man." He stood and buttoned his jacket. Looking down at me he said, "I'll see you tomorrow and we can continue this conversation."

CHAPTER TWENTY-ONE
RESCUE

My lack of knowledge seemed astounding. Not only were the last twenty or so days a blank, but that evening itself was a total mystery. I thought Malina was going to show up to bust me out. But I wasn't sure. Mulberry had made no mention of it, and I could tell that my brain was not working right.

But if I went with the assumption that Malina was going to bust me out of here tonight, the list of unknowns only grew longer. I didn't know what time Malina was going to show up, the layout of the floor I was on, how she planned to get us out of FGI headquarters. From the view I could tell we were very high up. There was a guard on my door. It wasn't locked, but when I tried to take a walk he insisted I stay in my room. Doctor's orders.

Dinner was brought to me by a young male orderly who smiled and asked how I was feeling. He set up the plate at a table in front of the TV and left me there to enjoy. I kept the TV off but ate the food. It was good. Steak and mashed potatoes with a salad. I ate it all and then the orderly came back and took away the tray. He was almost out the door when he noticed the steak knife was missing. He turned around and smiled at me and asked me to return it. I shrugged like I didn't know what he was talking about.

He smiled. "They will flip this room if you don't give it to me. Patients cannot keep weapons. I understand you're worried about your safety, but we are the best," he said with a reassuring smile. I pulled it out from under my pillow and gave it back.

Lying awake I stared up at the ceiling. There was a glass globe at its center. It was sandblasted opaque white and held in place by brass hooks. It was turned off but I kept the bedside lamp on. While the room shared the androgynous tone of an expensive hotel, the bed with its metal sides and panel of instruments instead of a headboard made it clear why people stayed here.

As I waited for the evening to unfold I sat cross legged on the bed, head bowed over linked hands and tried to remember. Later, I stood at the window and looked out onto the city, flipping through the cards in my head. Flickering images, crystal clear until the airboat bumped up against that cement dock. I could remember thanking Carl and them loading up their boat but it was fuzzy. Like I was watching it from under water.

I missed Blue. It felt like a wound in my chest. But when I inspected myself in the mirror there was nothing there. My body was pale, strong but pale. Like I hadn't been outdoors in awhile, eighteen days was my guess. There was more roundness to my hips and arms. This was what my body looked like when I relaxed, when the energy vibrating in me didn't use up every ounce of fuel I gave myself.

I was covered in healing cuts. The one on my forearm was the worst, but my calves and knees also looked like they'd been torn at. Thirty-six hours in the Everglades. Just me and Blue. Where did I get the cigarette from? That couldn't have been real.

By ten at night I was starting to feel edgy, pacing quietly, feeling Blue by my hip despite the fact that he wasn't there. There was a knock at my door. I stopped pacing and zeroed in on it. I heard the lock turn and then a nurse, one I hadn't seen before but wearing the same blue scrubs as the other, stepped in, keeping her hand on the knob. "You okay?" she asked. "Need something to sleep?"

I shook my head. "No, thank you."

She cocked her head. "All right, you want the TV on?"

"I think I'll just read," I said, not wanting the noises from the TV to distract me. It seemed harder to tell what was real when the TV was on.

She left and I climbed into bed, the pajamas I'd been given making me feel like a child. Matching top and bottoms in blue pinstripe, it was like a little suit. I had a robe, too. And slippers. I got back out of the bed and walked to the closet. Workout clothing. Not any I'd owned before. Pajamas. Jeans that looked like pajamas. Sweatshirts. Who the hell bought this stuff? Why would I be wearing this? This clothing belonged to an invalid. Why couldn't they have gotten me in some freaking real pants?

I closed the doors and went back to the bed. Wanting to change so that when Malina arrived I'd be ready but knowing that would seem strange. Then again, how could anything I do seem strange? I'll tell the nurse it makes me feel comfortable. No, the guard will know. But, he's not watching me, is he? My brain ran around like this, uncontrolled, garbled, until I decided it was time for some Tai Chi. After all, I was wearing the right outfit for it.

Facing the windows I took a cleansing breath and then began, conscious only of where I was in that moment. Feeling each breath wash through me, from my nose, into my lungs, filling my chest, pushing down my thighs, swirling around my knees, plunging past my calves and reaching to the very tips of my toes, bringing every vessel in my body to life, reminding it that we were here now, in this moment, and nowhere else.

Merl would be proud, I thought after four nice forms. My breathing was regulated, mind calmed, and body limber. It was midnight. I decided to sleep. As I laid down I told myself, Don't dream. Don't dream. Just rest.

EK

Malina picked me up in a red Mustang. She wore a tight white halter dress that showed off the caramel color of her skin. The car's top was down and she wore a scarf around her long hair. The nurse pushed me out in a wheelchair despite my protests. "You're looking pale," Malina said.

"Thanks," I said, climbing into the passenger seat, my limbs still heavy and cumbersome but slowly coming back to me. "I feel good," I said. And I did. I felt ready. "Let's go."

She pulled out of the parking lot and entered the highway, swerving between cars, her scarf streaming out behind her. We got off in the warehouse district and Malina pulled into a covered garage, driving up to the second floor and parking next to a black Lincoln with tinted windows. We got out of the Mustang and she locked it before placing the keys under the front tire. Then pulling a second set of keys out of her bag opened up the town car. The interior was all black leather and dark wood. She took off her scarf and threw it over the seat. Turning the car on she drove back down to street level.

EK

A sound at the door woke me up. Instantly I knew it was Malina, that it was time to go. There seemed to be the tinge of electricity in the air. The lock turned and Malina walked in. She was wearing a pair of silk shorts, strappy high heels, and a white blouse that her breasts pushed against.

When she saw me sitting at the edge of the bed, putting my feet into slippers, her eyes momentarily filled with tears; they reddened and her nose swelled. I saw it all from across the room. She turned away from me to close the door quietly and said,"Turn off the light." I reached across the bed and did as she asked, sinking the room into semi-darkness, the lights of the city still filling the space with a smoky glow. Malina crossed to my side. Up close I could see there was nothing but determination on her face, eyes clear, pouty lips set in a line.

"Stand up," she said.

My slippers were on so I did, but I was confused by her tone. "Follow me, stay right behind me. Do not—"

I held up a hand. "Malina," I said, "I think I know how to bust out of a golden cage. Don't worry."

"Oh Sydney," she said, throwing her arms around me.

"I doubt we have time for this," I said, embracing her back.

"They told me you were back but that you might not be when I came. I just, I hoped so much you'd be here." She pulled back from me, trying to control a smile. "We are going up to the roof, a helicopter is coming for us," she explained, remembering the serious nature of her visit.

"Great," I said. "Obstacles?" I asked as I headed toward the door.

"I took out your guard—" When I cocked my head in question she shook hers a little to tell me she didn't have time to explain and continued. "The nurses, but I don't think they will try anything." I nodded. "And the two men on the roof," she said, her hand on the knob.

"Armed?"

"Of course."

"What did you bring?"

She smiled. "My charm and a dart gun. Also, I don't think they can shoot you without Bobby killing them."

"We'll find out," I said. "You lead the way."

Malina nodded and I pulled open the door. The hallway was silent and my slippers made soft padding noises. Malina's cork wedges were almost as silent. As we reached a T in the hallway I heard the sound of two women talking. Blue's low growl came to my ears and I slowed my steps. Malina pointed to the left and mouthed "nurses'. She pointed right and we slid against the wall. Malina peeked left. I couldn't see what she was looking at, so when she waved me on I took it at blind faith that it was time to go. Malina dipped around the corner, staying close to the wall, her stride long but quiet.

I glanced left long enough to see the edge of a counter, one arm resting against it, the rest of the woman out of sight. Then mimicking Malina's gait, I followed her down the hall. She ducked into what I thought was a hallway leading left but turned out to be an alcove with large elevator doors set in it. Malina pulled a key out of her pocket and turned it in the wall. A soft whirr announced the elevator's imminent arrival.

The doors swooshed open revealing a space large enough to carry twenty people or two people on gurneys along with their attendants. We got in and Malina turned the key in the lock noted as for fireman use only. The doors closed and we started up.

"Where are the guards?"

"Not sure. I'm going to pretend to be a prostitute sent up by Murphy."

"Murphy?"

She looked over at me. "Your guard."

"Okay."

"I'll take the first one into the bathroom, knock him out, and then come back for the other."

"What do I do?"

"Hide in the ladies room?"

"Are you joking?"

Malina bit her lip. "When we came up with this plan you were comatose."

The elevator stopped. "Best to stick to the plan," Malina said as the doors opened. She stepped off and I followed. We were in a brightly lit hallway. Malina pointed to a ladies room sign. "Fine," I said and pushed through the doors. The bathroom was painted white with white tiles and two wooden stalls. Close to the door was a wooden bench. I sat on it and listened to one of the toilets running, it reminded me of something and I tried to ignore the thought, hoping it would ping into my mind.

I heard Malina's laugh and then the door of the men's room opened. One of the hinges needed oiling. I stood up and walked to the wall the two restrooms shared, placing my ear against the cool drywall. More laughter, a grunt, a stall door slamming open and then silence. I stepped to my exit and pushed the door so that I could see the men's room entrance. It opened wide and Malina stepped through, not even throwing a glance in my direction. I moved back into the bathroom and waited again.

How was she going to pull this off? The second guy wasn't going to come that easy, and had she hidden the first guy well enough? Have faith, I thought, but then I heard gunfire. I was halfway to the glass doors leading out to the helipad by the time I realized I'd left the bathroom. Slamming through the doors I scanned the rooftop wildly. Malina was there, her hair whipping in the wind, the body of a man at her feet.

EK

A spotlight hit her, and looking up I saw a small helicopter approaching. The rotors ripped through the air, sounding like thunder on the rooftop below. Malina grabbed my arm and pulled me toward the craft, her head low. I hunched over, copying her pose. Staring at the concrete I squinted my eyes against the dust blowing up from it.

The wind under the blades made it impossible to hear but Malina climbed aboard and then pulled me up alongside her. She pushed me into a chair and fastened my belt, the tip of her tongue poking out, her brow furrowed.

She slid into her own seat just as the helicopter lifted off the ground, ascending straight up and then banking east, toward the ocean. Once her seatbelt was secured Malina handed me a pair of headphones with a microphone that I slipped over my head. The noise was instantly muffled.

Malina put her headset on and set the microphone against her smiling mouth. The pilot's voice came over the headphones and my eyes jumped to the back of his head. Short blonde hair came to a point at the base of his neck. He turned toward me so that I could make out his profile, strong jaw, roman nose, a microphone curling around to touch pink lips.

"Welcome aboard, Miss Rye," he said with a smile before turning his attention back to the front. The buildings below seemed like trees reaching toward us, while a bank of clouds formed a ceiling above. I thought I saw lightning but didn't feel its pulse so wondered if I'd imagined it.

"Sydney?" Malina said. I jerked my attention back to her. 'You okay?"

I nodded. "Where are we going?" I asked.

"You remember my friend Lenox?"

"The man on the phone."

"Yes, he is expecting us." Malina smiled.

"What?"

"Everything will be explained soon," she said.

"Will Blue be there?"

She nodded. "Yes." Then Malina turned to look out the side, down onto the city below. I looked at my feet and saw that I'd lost a slipper along the way. I felt the vibrations of the helicopter through my bare foot. I could see that it was resting on metal but I felt soft, dead leaves tickling at my toes.

The trip was short—no more than ten minutes and we began to descend. We were lowering toward a helipad next to a marina. The boats bobbed gently in their slips. When we were ten feet from the ground the surface of the bay shimmered from our wind. With a soft jerk we landed.

Malina's seatbelt was off and she undid mine. I felt like a child as she pulled off my headset, the door opening. Our captain stood there, his back hunched forward, short hair flattened to his head. He held out a hand and I took it. Using him to steady myself, I climbed out of the helicopter, keeping my head low, glad to have my feet back on the ground.

He put his arm around my back and walked me out from under the blades. "Thanks," I said once we were far enough away to stand up tall and be heard.

"Happy to help," he said before hurrying back to his craft. Malina stood next to me, watching him climb in.

"Gorgeous, no?" she said.

He waved once before lifting the helicopter back into the air. "Yeah," I said. "Who is he?"

"A friend," she answered before taking my arm again. "We must keep moving."

"Where are we going?" I asked again.

"Trust me," she answered.

I followed her out an unlocked gate and through the marina where she used a keycard to gain access to one of the docks. We passed massive yachts, sparkling under the marina's lighting. They had names like "Botox Barbie" and "Never Enough". At the very end of the dock a massive boat loomed. It was three stories tall, white and black, sleek and fast looking. I was staring up at it when Malina called my attention to her. "

"Here," she said, pointing to a very small but awesomely cool boat resting in the shadow of the large one. It was squeezed in at the very end of the dock. Wooden, painted bright red, with a low windshield and two tan leather seats, it looked comfortable and fast. Malina undid her shoes and tossed them into the back before hopping aboard. The key was in the dash and she turned it over once, the boat revving to life with a small plume of smoke rising out its back end.

"Untie the lines," she said.

I kicked off my remaining slipper, tossing it in next to her shoes and then started on the lines. First the bow line, tossing it onto the deck. The boat began to drift off the dock ever so slightly. Hurrying, I unraveled the stern line and with it still in hand leapt into the small boat. It rocked as my weight hit but stayed steady. Malina steered us away from the dock and out into the bay. "Secure those lines," she said, not taking her eyes off the horizon.

I wound the thick rope around my elbow and over my thumb forming a loose oval before dropping it onto the deck and then climbed onto the front to do the same with the bow line. Malina smiled at me as I took the seat next to her and then pushed forward on the throttle. The little boat's bow rose out of the water, while the stern with its strong engine dipped lower and thrust us forward. Moving over the smooth surface, staying in the lines of a channel marked by glowing, bobbing buoys, we followed the path out toward the ocean.

"Malina?" I said.

"Yes?"

"Are we going through there?" I asked, staring at the narrow inlet we were zooming toward. Waves rolled up to the inlet and then curved up, foaming at the top, and broke, rushing into the bay in a turbulent mess.

"Yes," she said, her hands relaxed on the wheel, long hair blowing behind her, tangling in the rough air.

"Are those waves?"

Malina laughed. "Yes, Sydney, we are going into the ocean."

I nodded. "Okay."

Malina timed our exit from the safe waters of the bay into the deep blue of the ocean perfectly so that we raced through on a lull, rising up the next wave, caught air coming off its crest, and surfed down its back, up the next, and then we were out in the Atlantic.

The moon shone above us reflecting white off facets of the water's surface. The rest of the seascape was a rich black. Electric lights from other boats dotted the waterscape. The engine of our little boat roared and we raced up the long, large rollers and then down them. It was almost like driving between low hills. At certain moments, when we were at the base of one, the nose of our boat just beginning to climb, I couldn't see anything but walls of water around us, the clear black sky twinkling with stars above.

EK

"There it is," Malina said, pointing to a large yacht in the distance. As we got closer I could make out that it was strung with lights, the sound of music and laughter carrying across the water to us. Groups of people were on the decks. Some were dancing, others talked. They all seemed to be drinking.

"A party?" I asked.

"It's a cover," Malina yelled over the wind. She picked up the radio next to the steering wheel and hailed the ship. "This is Red Bird. Do you hear me Sea Dragon?"

The answer came back instantly and I recognized the accent, the sexy baritone, even over the crackling of the radio. "Yes, I see you Red Bird. Approach."

The music seemed to grow louder and people started flocking toward the bow of the boat as we approached the stern. Malina shifted into neutral and let the wind push us up to the swim deck where a man waited, a rope held loosely in his hand. He had olive skin, dark hair, and was wearing a sailor outfit more suited for a strip club than an actual vessel.

The sailor threw the line and I caught it. Malina pointed to a cleat in the center of the boat and I tied it off. Malina threw him our bow line and the sailor hauled us in using the two ropes and some pretty impressive biceps. His shirt was so tight I thought that his sleeves might burst. Malina threw small bumpers over the edge and we tapped against the swim platform gently. Looking up I saw a tall, broad man wearing a finely cut suit in dark blue looking over the railing at us. He smiled, exposing perfectly white teeth. His skin was deep black, the same rich color as pure cocoa powder.

The sailor offered his hand and I climbed out of the small boat, leaving my remaining slipper behind. The teak deck was cool and damp under my bare feet. He motioned to the metal ladder leading up to the deck and I grabbed at it, wrapping my hands around the cool rungs, excitement building as I remembered Blue was aboard.

When I reached the deck the man waiting held out his hand. I placed mine in his and he raised it to his lips. "I am Lenox," he said as his smooth lips brushed the back of my scarred hand. Without letting go of me he looked up, his brown eyes bright and excited looking. "It is my pleasure to have you aboard."

Malina climbed up next to me and laughed when she saw Lenox over my hand. "Come on," she said, grabbing my arm.

"Take me to Blue," I said. Malina nodded, leading me down the deck and to a wooden staircase. We climbed three levels to the top deck of the boat, Lenox right behind us. As we stepped back out onto the deck, I stopped and, holding onto the railing, looked down on the party below. Handsome sailors, dressed in whites, wandered around with trays of drinks and food. Well-built men, some in jeans, others in suits almost as nice as Lenox's, grinded on the dance floor with women who looked older and wealthier than their gyrating partners. Directly below me, on the second floor, a man and woman moved in the shadows, her moans only slightly louder than the slap of flesh.

Lenox stood next to me, his large hands wrapping around the railing close to mine. "Quite an operation you have here," I said. I heard the boat's engines start up and the sea behind the ship turned turbulent as she eased forward.

He smiled down at me. "Thank you."

"Come on," Malina said. She stood by an open door and I walked through. It was a ship's hallway, narrow and lined on one side with rounded doors, and on the other windows looking out to the passing ocean. "That one," Malina said, pointing to the last door. I turned the handle and heard an excited bark. When I opened the door Blue spilled out into the hall. I crouched down and he buried his head into my chest, crying once. Wrapping my arms around him I leaned my face in his fur. He whined again and I squeezed harder. "It's okay," I said. "Everything is okay."

Looking up I saw Merl standing in the well-appointed state room next to a double bed. His dogs sat around him. The puppy barked once at Blue, a sharp cry. But Michael, the largest dog, glared at the youth, who pinned his ears to the back of his head in apology.

Standing up I walked to Merl, Blue pressing against my hip. We embraced. "Thank you," I said.

"My pleasure," Merl answered.

I sat on the bed and Blue snuggled up to me. I petted his ears and kissed his snout, right below his eyes. "You are such a good boy," I told him. He closed his eyes and sighed appreciatively.

"Is everyone else here?" Malina asked.

"We're just waiting on Mulberry," Lenox answered.

"Sydney," Malina said. I looked up at her. "You want to get changed?" I laughed and nodded. She grinned. "I have some clothing for you there." She pointed at a built-in desk where a folded pair of jeans and a top sat. "I tried to get them to put you in something else at that place but was overruled." I laughed again. "What?" she asked.

Merl started for the exit, his dogs moving with him. "Let's give her a minute, come on," he said. They left and then it was just me and Blue in a strange room on a yacht full of male prostitutes. I slid onto the floor and sat down with Blue's head and chest in my lap. I stroked his face and whispered to him about how good he was and how much I loved him. I thanked him for saving my life, again.

There was a knock at the door and Blue quickly righted himself, standing next to me, his ears perked forward. Dan walked in. He hadn't shaved either and from the dark circles under his eyes it didn't look like he had slept much since I'd left him at his place in Key West. "Sydney," he said, smiling as he crossed the room. I stood up, using the bed to help. Dan leaned over me and, burying his face into my neck, wrapped his arms around my shoulders. I stroked his back. "I'm so glad you're back," he said.

"Thanks," I said. "You okay?" I asked.

He let go of me and smiled. "I am now," he said.

"Were you there when they found me?" I asked.

"I found you," he said, a frown pulling at the corner of his mouth. "Mulberry and I. Why didn't you tell either of us what you were doing?" he asked, his eyes dark and serious, almost angry, but he looked too tired to be angry.

"I thought I had it under control. Besides," I smiled, "aren't you always tracking me?"

Dan sat on the bed with a sigh. "Sydney, I track your phone. If you go for a swim with it in your pocket it stops working." He stared up into my eyes. "You scared the shit out of me."

"I'm sorry," I said, feeling it in my gut. While I tore myself apart trying to make sure no one I cared about got hurt when I put myself in danger, I hurt them just the same. Dan scratched at his beard. Blue leaned against me.

"I'll forgive you," he said. "But will you promise me something?"

"I'll try."

"Don't do anything like that ever again."

"I don't know what I did," I said with a weak smile. "How did you find me?" Fear flicked across Dan's face. "What?" I asked.

He licked his lips. "When I saw Blue I knew you were close."

"Saw him where?" I asked, reaching down and rubbing under Blue's chin.

"At the edge of an apple hammock. He barked at us."

"When was this?"

"You'd been missing for almost two days."

"How?" I asked.

"When Mulberry didn't hear from you, he called me. I tracked your car and he drove out there. Mulberry found Professor Nablestone's corpse. At that point the storm was really in full swing." I imagined Mulberry standing next to his car, the headlights illuminating a gruesome scene spread out across the cement launch area, lightning cracking around him as sheets of rain pelted the ground. "The storm kept us from searching much until it died down around dawn. Then Mulberry got helicopters in the air, men out on boats, we combed that swamp looking for you." He rubbed at his beard again.

"But it was you two who found me?"

"It was Merl's idea to call Blue."

I felt a tear in my eye. "And he came," I said, swiping at the tear. "He answered."

Dan smiled. "After almost two days of searching. I think it's my favorite sound that I've ever heard."

"Was I with him?"

Dan licked his lips. "You weren't with him, but we knew you were close. Mulberry and I barely fit between the tree trunks but Blue urged us forward, crying and barking until we reached you. I was in front and when I saw you there, curled up in a ball, lying on the ground holding the laptop case." He took a stuttered breath. "I just stopped and stared down at you. Blue sat next to you and whined at me. Then I saw your chest rise and I realized you were alive." Dan looked up at me. "But I was still so scared, Sydney. Mulberry and I both were. You were lying so still, and you were covered in mud and blood. And," he licked his lips again, "you were lying on a patch of ground. Blue had dug a bed for you, in the dirt, deep in the hammock." He paused for a moment looking down.

"What happened next?"

"I felt your neck." His gaze rose to my throat and he reached out, placing two fingers over my pulse. "And you were warm," he said with a smile. "And I could feel your heartbeat."

He kept his fingers against my skin. "When I bent down to pick you up your eyes opened and," he licked his lips, "you didn't see me, Sydney.

I don't know what you saw but you thought it was a threat. You kicked me in the ribs." He put his hand to his side. "So fucking hard."

"God, I'm sorry Dan," I said, leaning toward him. I tried to touch his side but he caught my hand. "It's okay," he said. "The crazy thing is, Blue stopped you."

"What do you mean?"

"He growled at you, and Sydney, you sat back down, turning to him, holding the laptop. That's when I realized what had happened to you."

"Datura."

"Mulberry told you to stand up and you did. I mean you'd do anything we told you to."

I shuddered at the thought. Dan squeezed my hand.

"We've tested your blood, and I managed to match what you were given to records in the laptop. You came out of the hallucinations without any memories within the timespan expected. You may have residual effects for another month or more."

"Residual effects?"

"Hallucinations, vivid dreams, maybe other things."

I bit my lip, letting the pain ground me for a moment. "Will I ever remember?" I asked, not sure what I wanted the answer to be.

"I don't know."

"You look tired," I said.

He laughed, "You should see yourself."

I shrugged. "Not my finest moment."

Dan laughed again. "I don't know," he said with a smile.

"Thank you," I said. "Thank you for finding me."

He leaned over and kissed my palm, his warm lips soft against my skin. There was a quick knock on the door and then it cracked open. "Are you decent?" Mulberry's voice asked.

"Come in," I said. Dan didn't let go of my hand. Mulberry walked in and stopped looking at us. He had shaved and wore a light jacket over a black and white checkered shirt. I thought he looked like the picture of Smooth Corporate Private Eye. But as he stared at our linked hands I saw the roughness inside him. The part of him that kept him from becoming too slick, too perfect.

"Sorry," he said. "Just wanted to see if you were ready. We've got a tight schedule." Mulberry forced a smile.

"Schedule?" I asked.

Dan stood. "Get changed and then come to the Captain's dining room. It's at the other end of the hall."

"What's going on?" I asked.

"It will all be explained," Dan promised.

"If we have time," Mulberry said, holding the door open.

CHAPTER TWENTY-TWO
JOYFUL JUSTICE

I changed quickly into the jeans, T-shirt, and hoodie that Malina had left for me. Tying the laces of the sneakers I felt the bass thrumming through the floor from the party down below. Blue's nose touched my hip rhythmically as I walked along the hall to the Captain's dining room. I took a deep breath, Blue warbled reassuringly. I reached out and opened the door.

Lenox, Malina, Merl, Mulberry, Dan, and Anita sat around an oval wooden dining table. The view of the ocean out the round portholes behind them shifted as the boat rose and fell. The murmur of conversation halted as they all turned to look at us.

Anita jumped up. She looked great, her skin clear, wearing a blue and white silk kurta that brushed at her knees with a pair of jeans and simple leather sandals. She threw her arms around me in a hug. "You look good," I said smiling. "I'm glad to see you so well."

"Thanks to you and Dan," she said, releasing me and looking over at him. He smiled back at us.

"What are you doing here?" I asked.

Dan answered. "This is the project I told you she was working on."

Mulberry cleared his throat. "She's been a great help to us. Anita designed our PR strategy."

I nodded, "Right," I said. "PR Strategy. Everyone's got to have one."

Mulberry cleared his throat again. "Come on, let's get started."

Anita returned to her seat. There were a couple of manila envelopes on the table in front of her. I sat between her and Malina. Mulberry was at the far end and Lenox at the other. Dan and Merl sat across the table from me.

"All right," Mulberry said. "Let's bring this meeting of the Joyful Justice council to order."

I laughed. Mulberry's eyes jumped to my face. "I'm sorry, Sydney," he said. He ran a hand through his hair. "We didn't expect you to be awake, but since you're here I thought you should sit in on the meeting."

"What is this?" I asked.

"Merl's in charge of combat," Mulberry said. "Dan is obviously the head of our technology department, Malina has been working on recruiting assets. Anita, PR. And Lenox is the head of our Miami chapter." I stared at him, my mouth slightly open, my brain slow and confused. "The whole reason we were taking you out tonight is because we are launching our first attack."

"Attack?"

Malina sat forward, a lock of her deep brown hair falling over her left shoulder as she did so. "Tonight, we will deal with Ivan Zhovra and let the world know that we are here. Once Ivan's strip clubs close for the night my girls will make their move. There are seven clubs in the area which the women are forced to work, but only four houses where they sleep. We have a plant in each house who will take out the guards with some outside assistance from us."

Anita interrupted and I turned to look at her. "Once the girls are free we've got vans to take them over to a church which will offer them asylum until proper documentation can be obtained."

Malina started up again. "Once the women are safe—"

"Wait," I asked. "Who are these shooters?"

"Women we've recruited to work for their own freedom. You met one of them."

I raised an eyebrow.

"The woman in the blue dress," Lenox said.

I remembered her pale skin against the dresses bright tone. The way it was a little loose on her thin frame and rustled slightly as she shook. The one who spoke English but wouldn't speak.

"What will they do? Go to the church and hope their act is seen as self defense?"

"No," Mulberry said.

"Where will they go?" I asked.

Dan answered me. "We'll fly them to our new training camp in Costa Rica."

My eyebrows raised. "You've been busy," I said.

He nodded. "Yes, we have."

Mulberry took control again, asking Merl to fill me in on what came next. "Each of the seven clubs are located in somewhat isolated areas. They are all free-standing buildings with no close neighbors. So," Merl said, "we are going to blow them up."

"Wow," I said.

A boyish smile appeared on Merl's face for a second and then disappeared just as quickly. "No one will get hurt," he assured me.

"Then what happens?" I asked.

"They have a choice," Mulberry said.

"What?"

"Change their ways."

"Or what?"

Merl answered. "The best threats are those imagined in your opponent's mind."

"Besides," Dan said, "with the testimony of the freed women it shouldn't be hard to prove human trafficking and a host of other crimes."

I nodded. "Okay, saving the enslaved women, blowing up the clubs, giving the bad guys an ultimatum. I like it so far, what's next?"

Anita answered me. "That's the best part." She pushed a single typed page across the table to me.

I looked it over. "Joyful Justice takes full responsibility," "Slavery in plain sight," "Not going to take it anymore," "Justice will be served," and at the bottom, "Joyfuljustice.com Join the revolution."

"Wow," I said again, my heart beating hard.

"What do you think?" Anita asked. She was biting her lip and looking at me for my approval.

What could I say? "Great," I answered. "Perfect." She smiled. When I pushed the paper back to her, my fingers trembled slightly.

"This will go out to every major news venue," Anita said, returning the paper to one of her files. "And we will release video confessions after the attack from the women leading the escape in Ivan's houses."

"Sounds almost like terrorism," I said.

Anita nodded. "I'm using a lot of their tricks against them," she said. "Soon, anyone who thinks they can take advantage of those weaker than them will see what the meek can do." A fire burned in her eyes as she spoke and I could feel her passion and her faith. It frightened me.

"Sydney," Mulberry said. "We should talk about your role."

I nodded turning to him. "Great. What can I do?"

He pursed his lips. "Leave." He held up a hand to block my protest. "Sorry, Sydney, but you're too exposed. And you don't need to be here."

"But I can help," I said.

"Bobby Maxim is going to lose it when he realizes what we're doing here." He put a finger against the polished wood table.

"You think he'll try to kill me?"

"More like he'll bring Joy back from the dead."

I laughed and Mulberry's brow furrowed. "He did threaten to do that," I admitted.

"See," Dan said, sitting forward. "You've got to go."

"Where?" I asked. "Where do you want me to go?"

"Costa Rica," he said.

Malina jumped in. "You'll love it, Sydney. It's all set up. Wait until you see it."

"You're stashing me at the training camp?" I asked. "Don't you think I'm more useful in a fight than most of the people at this table."

They all looked at each other, none of them at me. Lenox spoke for the first time. "You must recover, Sydney," his voice was soft but penetrating. I looked over at him. He was nodding at me. There was a knock at the door. "Come," Lenox said.

It was a sailor, he was tall and broad, his skin tan against the white of his uniform. "The launch is ready," he said. Lenox stood. "Sydney, it's time to go."

Anita stood up and pulled me from my chair into an embrace. Malina hugged me next, then Merl and Dan came around the table. Each enveloped me with their own scent and warmth for a moment.

I felt the ground tremble beneath me and heard the rumble of thunder pass through the space. Blue leaned against my hip sensing that something was wrong. "Are you okay?" Mulberry asked, reaching for my arm, holding me steady. The thunder disappeared.

"Yes," I said.

"I'll walk you down," he said, keeping hold of me as we moved toward the door.

"Thank you, Lenox," I said.

He bowed gracefully. "I am at your service."

EK

We walked back down the stairs, the thumping of the party the only noise. He stopped at the bottom and looked through the porthole to the back deck. He turned to face me in the small space. 'You'll go by boat to Cuba and then we have a plane waiting for you," Mulberry said.

"When will I see you again?"

He smiled. "We'll all be down in Costa Rica soon," he said. "For the next meeting of the Joy—"

I cut him off by placing a finger to his lips. "Just don't say it," I said with a small smile.

Mulberry embraced me, I wrapped my arms around his neck, holding him close. His hands splayed across my lower back and I felt his heart beating. He kissed my neck and loosened his grip but I didn't let go. I pulled him closer, pressing my face into his chest, making light dance behind my closed lids, feeling safe and sound and not wanting to let go of the comfort of him.

Mulberry pulled me tighter against him, his breath in my hair, his lips at my ear. "I—" he whispered but didn't continue.

"I'll miss you," I said against his chest, the words coming out sloppy but true, making my heart rise into my throat.

"Oh Sydney," Mulberry said, burying his face into my neck and kissing me over and over again. His hand cupped the back of my head and he held me still, looking down at my face. "I'll miss you, too," he said, "I've *missed* you." His one hand held my head, the other pressed against my lower back, holding my entire body against his making it impossible to escape his gaze.

"Be safe," I said.

He promised he would.

EK

I was in the air when it happened. The whole thing, not a hitch, and I was 30,000 feet above the surface of the earth. I sipped champagne and watched the news on a flat screen TV.

A group calling itself Joyful Justice has taken responsibility for seven explosions around Miami Dade County tonight. While they call themselves revolutionaries, many are calling them terrorists.

My phone rang. "Bobby," I said. "How unexpected."

"What is this?" His voice was even and cold.

"I think that's been made clear by our press release."

"You think this will work? That you're going to change the world? Make it a better place?" His voice was so even I felt a chill run down my spine and was glad we weren't face to face.

"I'm willing to try."

"You should have joined me when you had the chance. I'll destroy you." His tone never changed. The man could have been offering me eggs.

"Maybe it's the other way around," I said, making sure to keep my voice just as even, just as calm, in a way, just as crazy. "You should think about joining me. I could use a man with your connections."

He laughed, low and sultry. "You can't run forever, Joy."

"My name is Sydney Rye, and I'm not running, Bobby, I'm leading." I hung up the phone and then sipped from my glass, the bubbles tickling my nose. Blue rested his head onto my knee and I used my free hand to pet one of his velvety ears.

EK

Turn the page to read an excerpt from
Inviting Fire, Sydney Rye Mysteries Book 6, or purchase it now and continue reading Sydney's next adventure: emilykimelman.com/IF

EK

Sign up for my newsletter and stay up to date on new releases, free books, and giveaways:
emilykimelman.com/News

Join my Facebook group, *Emily Kimelman's Insatiable Readers,* to stay up to date on sales and releases, have exclusive giveaways, and hang out with your fellow book addicts: emilykimelman.com/EKIR.

SNEAK PEEK
INVITING FIRE, SYDNEY RYE MYSTERIES BOOK 6

An almost silent moan passed between my parted lips. I needed to be quiet because no one could know. But it hurt. And it felt so good. His hand grazed against my throat, fingers wrapping around and entwining into the hair at the base of my neck. A tug and I arched my back, bending it so that our bodies stayed melted together as he kissed along my collarbone. He pulled my hair and I strained to follow his lead, my mouth opening wider.

"Say my name," he whispered against my skin. When I didn't he pinched me, squeezing my flesh between his strong fingers. I gasped. "Say it," he demanded.

"No," I answered.

Sharp pain twisted through me, electric and pleasurable. His tongue licked my ear, pulling the lobe between his teeth. "Say my name," he whispered, his lips moving over my sensitive flesh. "Say it or die."

"Never."

I woke up tangled in my sheets, Blue standing next to the bed, his eyes glowing green in the dark room. He whined at me gently. "I'm okay," I told him. He pushed his nose against the mosquito net and whined again. "You don't think so?" I asked with a small laugh.

He circled around to the net's opening. I sat up and reached through, petting his head to reassure him. Blue was a giant of a dog with one brown eye and one blue. When I adopted him he was tall, the height of a Great Dane, but thin. Still a puppy really. The pound in Bushwick, Brooklyn thought he was about a year old at the time.

Over four years later, Blue looked very different. His coat, which had been ratty when I brought him home to my apartment in Park Slope, now shone in the soft light of my bedroom. He had the markings of a wolf. Black and white and beige all sharing space on his large form. His snout was long and made me think there was some collie in his ancestry. Blue's chest was broad and strong. The pink scars that marked the entrance and exit wounds from a bullet Blue took for me were hidden beneath his long coat.

My scars from that battle were more obvious. One ran under my left eye. White and pink it arched across the top of my cheekbone, puckering the skin. Above that eye another scar, fainter than the first, ran across my forehead, slicing through my eyebrow and disappearing into my hair.

I wore my bangs long, covering the top scar. They almost reached to my gray eyes, but I made sure they never got in the way. My hair was black and cut short, barely reaching my chin. The heat here was too much to bother with long locks.

I looked out the glass doors of my balcony and into the jungle. The sky was still dark, the foliage a pitch black mass. I heard the guttural roar of the howler monkeys and knew the sun would be here soon. Blue's nails clicked against the tile floor as he walked to the door.

Blue stared at me, then looked at the door, then to me again. "I get it," I said. "You want to go for a run." He lowered his front end, waving his tail around in the air and let out a low warble. Some things would never change.

Throwing off the sheet, I climbed through the opening of my mosquito net. The tiles were cool against my bare feet. I dressed quickly, Blue following me around the room, encouraging me by tapping his wet nose against my hip.

Sneakers tied, headlamp in place and iPod in hand, I opened my bedroom door. The villa was dark. My house-mate, Cynthia Dawlings, was still in bed. The sky outside the glass was just turning a milky gray. As I closed the door behind me another group of howler monkeys began their morning call. These were closer and I could feel the force of their voices vibrate through me. The loudest land mammal on the planet, the howler monkey's roar can be heard up to three miles away through thick jungle foliage. These guys were in the tree behind my house, and I figured that Cynthia was probably waking up right about now.

As Blue and I started down the path toward the trails, I heard another group of monkeys start up in response to the ones in my yard. And then another, like a round robin of roars. The path we walked on was lit by low lights, yellow and solar powered. The air was moist and fresh--it carried a chill that wouldn't last long once the sun rose. I passed other villas on my route. This was once an eco-resort. Now it was a training center for Joyful Justice, the stupidest named organization to ever blow shit up. But no one asked me when they were naming it, even though I inspired the whole damn thing.

Blue touched my hip, pulling me away from my thoughts and back into the world we walked through. We passed the pool where guests used to sunbathe and read books. It was divided into lanes for swimming laps, the deck spotted with exercise equipment. The large lawn was used as a sparring grounds. Merl, one of the founding members of the Joyful Justice council, and the man who had trained me to fight, was there. He wore all black, the romantic light of dawn highlighting his shape against the dark trees beyond. The sword in his hand glinted as he swung it through the air.

Three dark shapes hunkered in the grass around Merl's moving form. Doberman Pinschers. Michael, the largest and strongest of the pack, stood as we approached. He let out a low growl, warning of our passing. Merl's eyes followed the sound and found me. He nodded without breaking stride, lowering into a deep squat and pulling his sword back, preparing to run through an imaginary opponent. His youngest dog, Chula, wagged his tail but stayed in the down position. The bitch of Merl's pack lay next to him, her head between her paws, ears swiveling, searching for anything her master might need to know.

I clicked on my headlight as I stepped into the jungle. Nature walks once used for tourist enjoyment served as my running route along with the crisscross of trails that connected our lookout posts. The gray light haunting the horizon didn't penetrate the thick foliage, so I needed the electric light. Turning on my iPod I picked up my pace, keeping it steady though, refusing to let the beat push me forward at a pace I could not maintain.

That was what I was doing in every part of my life. Or trying to. I needed to slow down, stop letting outside forces push me into actions that wiped me out. I liked to run at this hour. When the jungle seemed like a dense wall of nothing rather than the intensely alive and intertwined ecosystem that it was. With headphones on the darkness served as a blinder for me. It was good for the brain.

And my brain needed all the help it could get. Three months earlier I'd been doused with the hallucinogen datura. Sometimes called the Devil's Snare or Angel's Trumpet, it comes from the seeds of the Jimson Weed. Bell shaped and beautiful, the flower grows all over the world. The seeds, whether swallowed whole or brewed into a tea, cause nightmare hallucinations impossible to distinguish from reality. When processed into a powder, datura can be blown into your victim's face, leaving him conscious and completely pliable - or dead if you get the dose wrong.

The stuff that got me was developed in a lab, created as a sophisticated weapon. It entered through my eyes and I don't remember a thing. Thank God Blue was with me. He killed my attacker and led me into the Everglades where he kept me alive for almost two days before we were rescued. Dan, my ex-something, and Mulberry, my, oh jeez, something else, I guess, found me. I didn't return to consciousness for another 18 days. My friends had faith I'd come out of it. But no one knew for sure if my recovery would ever be complete. I still saw lightning and heard the clap of thunder on sunny days.

I ran faster, not wanting to think about the dreams. I hadn't had a night of peace since waking up. The man who haunted my sleep, playing with my body until I woke up desperate for release, didn't deserve my days, too. I told myself it was the datura. I didn't want to feel this way, to be so turned on by the hate I felt. But deep down, in the most primordial dangerous part of my brain I knew I liked it. I knew I needed it. I would die without it.

The music changed and I slowed my pace, noting that I was closing in on the first watchtower. Blue left my side, pulling out ahead, going to meet the dog who patrolled this area. He disappeared beyond the globe of light my headlamp threw. The property was ringed with zip-lines, a classic tourist attraction in Costa Rica. It let people get some time in the treetops, which were a different world than the ground I ran upon. We used those platforms to keep watch. Make sure no one was sneaking up on our little vigilante training ground.

Blue returned and got back into line, even with my hip. As we reached a hill, I couldn't help but speed up. My feet dug into the soft ground, my vision concentrating on the uneven path ahead, breath even, steady. This was what would save me, I thought. Persistence.

As I crested the hill I slowed, taking a moment to admire the view, turning around in a circle. I pulled my headphones off my ears and listened to the sound of the jungle waking up. The birds singing to the sun, encouraging its approach. The final calls of the nocturnal animals as they settled down for a day of rest. The wind rustling the leaves in the treetops. I took in deep lungfuls of air, smelling the mix of rot and sweetness that permeated the jungle. Life and death, all right here, hiding in the dark. Hiding in me.

Continue reading *Inviting Fire*: emilykimelman.com/IF

Sign up for my newsletter and stay up to date on new releases, free books, and giveaways:
emilykimelman.com/News

Join my Facebook group, *Emily Kimelman's Insatiable Readers,* **to stay up to date on sales and releases, have exclusive giveaways, and hang out with your fellow book addicts:** emilykimelman.com/EKIR.

AUTHOR'S NOTE

Thank you for reading my novel, *The Devil's Breath*. I'm excited that you made it to my "note". I'm guessing that means that you enjoyed my story. If so, would you please write a review for *The Devil's Breath*? You have no idea how much it warms my heart to get a new review. And this isn't just for me, mind you. Think of all the people out there who need reviews to make decisions. The children who need to be told this book is not for them. And the people about to go away on vacation who could have so much fun reading this on the plane. Consider it an act of kindness to me, to the children, to humanity.

Let people know what you thought about *The Devil's Breath* on your favorite ebook retailer.

Thank you,

Emily

ACKNOWLEDGMENTS

Thank you to my cousin, William Edwards, and his awesome wife, Natalia, for all their help with my Miami research. They let me crash at their gorgeous home, took time out of their busy lives to show me around, and answered all my questions. William even took me shooting! Thanks so much you two!

I also need to thank my friend, Mette Hansen Karademir. Without her none of my books would see the light of day. She is the perfect first editor, tough but sweet. She doesn't let me get away with anything…especially not believing that all my stuff is crap :)

My father, Donald Kimelman, has become a wonderful resource for me since his retirement and I feel very lucky to have such a great editor in the family. He helped to tighten up this book so that it shines. And he really doesn't let me get away with anything.

One last shout out to Gator Mike, who took me into the Everglades on his airboat and showed me the best places to dump a body. He also taught me that Gators won't eat us. We're too salty.

ABOUT THE AUTHOR

I write because I love to read...but I have specific tastes. I love to spend time in fictional worlds where justice is exacted with a vengeance. Give me raw stories with a protagonist who feels like a friend, heroic pets, plots that come together with a BANG, and long series so the adventure can continue. If you got this far in my book then I'm assuming you feel the same...

Sign up for my newsletter and
never miss a new release or sale:
emilykimelman.com/News

Join my Facebook group, *Emily Kimelman's Insatiable Readers,* to stay up to date on sales and releases, have exclusive giveaways, and hang out with your fellow book addicts: emilykimelman.com/EKIR.

If you've read my work and want to get in touch please do! I loves hearing from readers.
www.emilykimelman.com
emily@emilykimelman.com

facebook.com/EmilyKimelman
instagram.com/emilykimelman

EMILY'S BOOKSHELF

Visit www.emilykimelman.com to purchase your next adventure.

EMILY KIMELMAN
MYSTERIES & THRILLERS

Sydney Rye Mysteries

Unleashed

Death in the Dark

Insatiable

Strings of Glass

Devil's Breath

Inviting Fire

Shadow Harvest

Girl with the Gun

In Sheep's Clothing

Flock of Wolves

Betray the Lie

Savage Grace

Blind Vigilance

Fatal Breach

Undefeated

Relentless

Brutal Mercy

Starstruck Thrillers

A Spy Is Born

EMILY REED

URBAN FANTASY

Kiss Chronicles

Lost Secret

Dark Secret

Stolen Secret

Buried Secret

Date TBA

Lost Wolf Legends

Butterfly Bones

Date TBA

Made in the USA
Middletown, DE
08 September 2024

60403393R00149